FREMONT F. ELLIS

LAST OF *LOS CINCO PINTORES* OF SANTA FE

FREMONT F. ELLIS

LAST OF *LOS CINCO PINTORES* OF SANTA FE

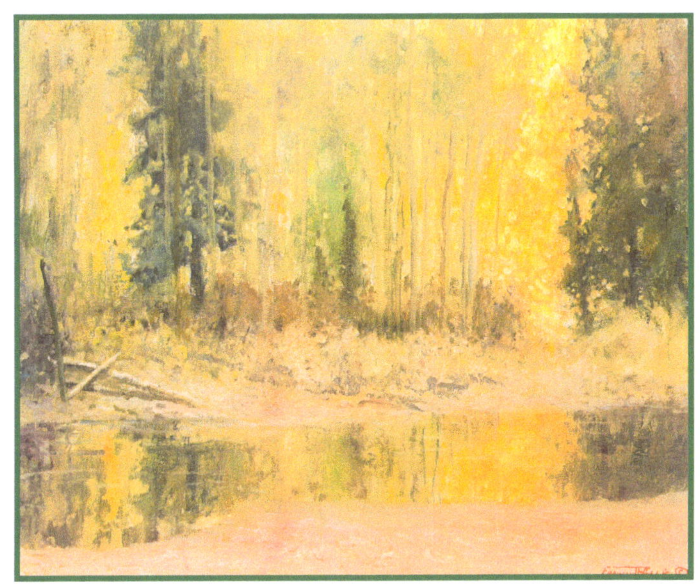

Barbara Spencer Foster

with

Bambi Elizabeth Ellis

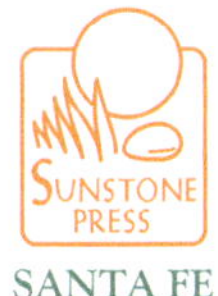

SANTA FE

Sunstone books may be purchased for educational, business, or sales promotional use. For information please write: Special Markets Department, Sunstone Press, P.O. Box 2321, Santa Fe, New Mexico 87504-2321.

Book and Cover design ›Vicki Ahl
Body typeface ›Goudy Old St BT

Library of Congress Cataloging-in-Publication Data

Foster, Barbara Spencer, 1927-
Fremont F. Ellis : last of Los Cinco Pintores of Santa Fe / by Barbara Spencer Foster with Bambi Elizabeth Ellis.
p. cm.
ISBN 978-0-86534-632-1 (softcover) ISBN 978-1-63293-426-0 (hardcover)
1. Ellis, Fremont F., 1897-1985. 2. Landscape painters--United States--Biography. I. Ellis, Fremont F., 1897-1985. II. Ellis, Bambi Elizabeth. III. Title. IV. Title: Last of Los Cinco Pintores of Santa Fe.
ND237.E553F67 2010
759.13--dc22
[B]

2010030297

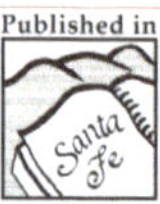

WWW.SUNSTONEPRESS.COM
SUNSTONE PRESS / POST OFFICE BOX 2321 / SANTA FE, NM 87504-2321 /USA
(505) 988-4418 / ORDERS ONLY (800) 243-5644 / FAX (505) 988-1025

Dedicated to Fremont F. Ellis whose appreciation and love for the enchanting beauty of the American Southwest inspired his majestic landscape paintings. His artistic brilliance was enhanced by the honor and modesty of a true gentleman.

—Barbara Spencer Foster

Dedicated to the family of Bambi Elizabeth Ellis; my daughter, Anna Karen Turner Evans; my son-in-law, Dr. Robert Evans; my grandchildren and my great grandchildren; also my brother, Frederick F. Ellis and his family.

—Bambi Elizabeth Ellis

CONTENTS

TRIBUTE

by

Tom Lea

I think I was set up for believing Santa Fe was something special. It is probable that I was "predisposed," as they say, to believe Santa Fe was for a fact a Capitol of a Land of Enchantment. Of course, I saw it first at a wonderful time. It was a flavorous old town of about ten thousand permanent residents with none of them seeming to be in much of a hurry. There were no crowds of tourists, no traffic lights, no gasoline engine stinks, few paved streets, only an occasional Indian in sight, and motels hadn't even been invented yet. I'll swear the old Plaza was not only a venerable but a quiet kind of place.

In the summer of 1922, I was fifteen years old, and going to be a junior at El Paso High that fall. I was also the earnest owner and blundering operator of a box of oil paints, and I was possessed of a desire deeply dyed, oh a serious desire, to become an artist. The real thing. Someday a painter of note.

There was, I realized, a lot I didn't know about it. In all my life, for instance, I had never yet set foot in a museum of art. Where I lived there was no such thing. Moreover, I had never yet had the privilege of meeting, or talking to, or being able to see inside the studio of a real artist—a pro—a working pro. With a north light, and a big daub-marked steady easel, and a palette set with a rainbow of bright colors, and a whole bunch of hog bristle brushes sticking up out of a jar on a work table, and canvases stacked, face to the wall.

Santa Fe was my chance!

I was on a motor trip with my folks, and we were staying at the DeVargas Hotel for a couple of days while my dad took care of some legal business for New Mexico clients. For me, it turned out to be a memorable time! I did set foot in a museum of art. And the next day I met, and I talked to, and I saw the studio of, a real artist, a working pro—a painter by the name of Fremont Ellis.

Thinking back, three score and seven years later, I can remember that I was excited, and also uncertain inside myself about myself, walking alone under the long portal in front of the Palace of the Governors, headed for the Museum of Art on the next block down the street. I can remember some hollyhocks in the sun by an adobe-colored wall, and walking in the Museum's wood-carved door, and feeling all of a sudden what a lot I had to learn; and I wished, how I wished, I could paint like that! Seeing the originals—not just reproductions in a book or magazine—of oil paintings, watercolors, pastels, framed drawings, wood blocks, matted etchings, I stayed looking, from way back, and from as close as my eyes could get, till long after noon. In one of the galleries, I eavesdropped. Two fellows stood arguing; at least they were both trying to make a point, in front of what seemed to me to be a modernistic-looking water color, a landscape. One fellow had a yellowish beard (in those days there weren't many beards around), and looked like he had on an old ratty pair of pink bedroom slippers. No socks. I kept hearing the words, "significant form." The loud-voiced fellow had on what was called a Windsor flowing tie, emerald green, and looked kind of like a seedy city dude in a big cowboy hat. Artists, for sure—maybe even famous ones.

There was a very nice lady at the desk where I bought some postcards of paintings before I left. I asked her if she could tell me where I could go to see an artist's studio. She must have been amused. She said I ought to go up the Camino del Monte Sol: there were some new adobe studios up there built by some very interesting young artists. They were a group calling themselves Los Cinco Pintores—the Five Painters, she translated, not knowing I was a border town Texan from El

Paso. I was embarrassed to ask her how to get to the Camino del Monte Sol, but it stayed in my mind—Road of the Sun Mount. In a town named Holy Faith. At the foot of the Blood of Christ Mountains. Whew!

That evening we had dinner with Dad's friend, Federal Judge Colin Neblitt, and he told me how to go if I wanted to get from the DeVargas to the Camino del Monte Sol up on the edge of town.

"Santa Fe, bless its old haht, is changing," I heard the Judge tell my dad. "We now have ah-teests all aboot us" (he was from Virginia). "Some very good, I unduhstand. And some—but I know not a dahmed thing aboot aht." And I heard my dad say, "Young Tom seems crazy about it."

Next morning I did find the place where you turned right and began heading uphill along the pair of wheel ruts that a man said, "Yup it's the Cumeenah Monty Sole awright; used to be called Telephone Road." The houses strung up the road were most all of them built on the right hand side, and I walked clear up to where there were no more houses just open ground speckled with pinon and cedar sloping east up to the pine timbered Sangre de Cristos.

I've gone past Los Cinco Pintores, I thought. And what a view! I stood across the road from the last house for a long time, up there in the quiet, looking around.

There was a shine, a silvery sort of radiance, in air scented faintly with wood smoke and pinon and cedar boughs warm in the sun. A man without a hat came from around the back of the last house up there on the Camino. I can't remember now exactly what was said, but it went very much like this:

"Looking for someone?"

"Oh, no sir. I was just looking."

He was wearing a flannel shirt and khaki riding pants and scuffed lace-up boots. His belt was real long and the end hung down, dangling from the buckle. He was built slight and spry looking, flat-bellied, and hardly any taller than I was.

"It's sure keen up here," I said, a little apologetic.

His face was clean shaven, but his brownish blonde hair was noticeably long, combed in a pompadour straight back over the top of his head, clear down to the collar at the back of his neck.

"What brought you?" he asked. He looked good humored asking.

"The lady at the Museum told me about Los Cinco Pintores and—I believe he must have noticed how I pronounced the Spanish and used 'Los' instead of 'The.'"

"Where you from?"

"El Paso."

"I lived down there for a while. You paint?"

"I wish I could paint."

"What's your name?"

I told him, and he said, "I'm Fremont Ellis. I live here." He indicated it with his thumb.

"You're one of the five painters?"

"Right. We exhibit together."

"Gee."

"Well," he said, "would you like to come in? See what I'm doing?"

"Would I? Oh, man!"

We walked into a room maybe not as big and more cluttered, but absolutely like I had figured a real studio: the north light, easel with painting on it, great big thumb-hole palette all spread with color, work table cluttered, wadded up paint rags, brushes all sizes, canvasses face to the wall—and something I hadn't imagined so much: the aromatic scent of spirits of turpentine with cold pressed linseed oil and damar varnish. It seemed like incense to me, standing there.

The painting on the easel was contrasty darks and lights: stormy sky with a shaft of sunlight hitting a hillside beyond a row of dark cottonwoods, and the shadowy shape of a long wall and adobe house with a dark door in the foreground. Moody. All with big brush strokes and thick paint.

I didn't know what to say about it without showing ignorance, so I said, "It's really swell."

"Needs work. The foreground," Fremont Ellis said. "You paint in oils?" He had gray-blue eyes looking straight in my face.

"I try." I said. It gave me my chance to say something. "But oil paint doesn't handle like I want, hardly ever. It gets sort of muddled. The lights get darkened, and the darks get lightened some way."

"I bet you're putting on the paint too thick and then fussing with it on the canvas. Lots of beginners are afraid to use the paint. They thin it and then use it like they're scared they'll run out. Then they see it on the canvas weak—and often in the wrong place, too—and they try to correct it by piling on more thin paint until the tone gets lost, and you have to scrape the whole thing off and start over—the main thing, handling oil paint, you got to keep it decisive! *Crisp*, see? You think what you're gonna do before you do it. You mix exactly the color you want, and plenty of it, on the palette and only then do you load the brush and stroke it on the canvas exactly where you have already decided it has to go. Crisp, see? Like that raw sienna and white on that hillside area here. And then leave it! Don't start monkeying with it! Crisp, see? Did you bring any of your work here with you?"

"No, sir."

"Next time you come, you let me see something, will you?"

It was about noon when I went walking down the Sun Mount Road from Mr. Fremont F. Ellis' studio, headed toward town and the DeVargas Hotel, and El Paso tomorrow—and my paint box. The elixir and the enchantment in the Santa Fe air that day blended *CRISP*, see, with the incense and the magic of painting pictures, and it all gripped my soul.

I managed brief returns to Santa Fe during the next two summers, and of course, I went up to see Fremont Ellis. I never got the nerve to show him one of my paintings, but I did show him drawings in my sketch book and some prints of linoleum blocks I made. He treated me like an adult. He even made me feel like a fellow artist as I looked at the landscapes he took the time and trouble to put on the easel to show me.

It was a deeply felt experience for me, knowing this painter in Santa Fe, seeing how he studied, how he struggled to show with the pigments on his palette how he loved the light and the look of the grand world he lived in.

Santa Fe stayed special, with a grip on my soul, during the eight years I lived away from my native Southwest.

One winter's day in Chicago, in a steam-heated studio on North Clark Street, three snow-crusted gray city blocks from an iced-over gray river, I whittled shavings, sharpening a drawing pencil into an empty tin watercolor pan. I put a match to the little pile of cedar wood shavings and it burned there in the quiet, a thin poignant whiff to remember: faraway wood smoke, tinged faintly with pinon and cedar warmed in the sun.

Early in 1933, in the very depths of the Great Depression, my wife, Nancy—she was an unpublished writer—and I decided it was about time for us to leave Chicago and head west. We had nearly a thousand dollars in savings from my work as an assistant in John Norton's mural studio, and we used it—we thought very carefully—to grub stake a home and an entirely new way of living, in Santa Fe, New Mexico, a place we had dreamed of for a long time.

Fremont Ellis no longer lived in his house on the Camino. He had moved to the new more spacious studio home he had built about ten miles south of Santa Fe, on a property he had acquired and named Rancho San Sebastian, some three hundred acres of hilly pinon and cedar country on the Vegas Road close by the Lamy cut-off.

There at the Rancho, upon a four-acre site Nancy and I chose and which Fremont provided—on credit—we built what we could barely afford, a one-room adobe house-studio, up on the ridge of a thickly wooded hill about a half mile of rocky road from where Fremont lived with his beautiful Latin wife, Lencha, and his two endearing children, Bambi and Freddy.

Our new home boasted no utilities. Not a single pipe or wire connected it with 'civilization.' But it had a view, a sublime view, looking out upon a hundred leagues of unpeopled and untroubled mountain and plain and blue distance under a majestic dome of sky. There were stars in our eyes, brushes and pens and notebooks in our hands, and great hopes in our hearts then, living in our house on the hill.

There was the matter of having to make a living. Shortly after arrival in Santa Fe, I had the luck of landing a part time job as an artist-draftsman on the staff of the Laboratory of Anthropology in town. Though it kept me from total devotion to my own sketchbooks and paint box, it and a few other providential odd jobs put enough chow on our lean hilltop table to keep us going and growing.

In town, times were tough. For most artists those days, selling a picture was practically out of the question. Fremont Ellis was an exception. Even in Depression Days, we saw him manage to provide for his family and himself the kind of life he wanted to live, by selling or trading his paintings—without deviating from his own intent course as a dedicated artist. Art circles in town were heard using the term 'pot boiler' referring to the often repeated theme of golden aspens or fall-time cottonwoods in many Ellis paintings. In our view from the hill, we found some aesthetic snobbery and a grain of covert envy involved in this disdain expressed for a man who painted pictures people often liked so well they bought them.

We shared happy times on the Rancho San Sebastian with the Ellis family, all four of them. We became close friends. The wives, Lencha and Nancy, liked each other, and this strengthened the friendship between Fremont and me. We were often at each other's tables and in each other's studios. We watched each other's work, and we listened to what each other had to say about things in general and things in particular.

Up there on our hill with a view in a land we believed enchanted, Nancy and I felt that we had found the right place, that we were now doing the right thing with our lives and with the work that enthralled us—until Nancy fell ill, and at the hospital in Santa Fe underwent surgery for acute appendicitis, and never recovered.

After more than a year of illness, she died in an El Paso hospital on the first of April in 1930.

Three weeks after her death, I went up the hill to the house, loaded some things I wanted on a pickup truck, left the house key in the lock on the door and drove away. I never went back. I never saw Fremont Ellis again. In May of 1936, I began life and work again in El Paso where I was born.

In all the years of my life, I think I never met a man so in love with painting, the physical act of painting, as Fremont Ellis. He loved the very pigments he squeezed from tubes to his palette. He was deeply enamored of the very exercise of painting, of the heft and feel of a loaded brush touching in just the right place upon the textured surface of taut, inviting canvas. The whole magic of the act of painting he loved with hand and heart, the magic of making colors and tomes into depths of space and illusions of light upon the blank flatness of a surface merely two dimensional.

In love with paint, he was also in love with the land where he lived. He was not a portraitist, not a figure painter; he was a landscapist. His grand subject was Earth outdoors, under the light of the open sky; for him, a particular piece of Earth, under the light of a particular sky, the mountains and plains, the hills and valleys, the mesas and gulches, the settlements with their adobe walls under the trees by running water, the cornfields and horse pastures, the aspens and the pines, and small mankind under the light of heaven. Northern New Mexico. In daylight and dark, in storm or shine in summer, winter spring or fall, for sixty-seven painting years he felt the land's enchantment. He put his skill as a painter with his love for the looks and the moods of the land he lived in, and left us some superb pictures of it.

I believe that Fremont Ellis addressed his deepest feelings about the Almighty and His handiwork—with a paint brush in his hand.

—Tom Lea
December, 1989

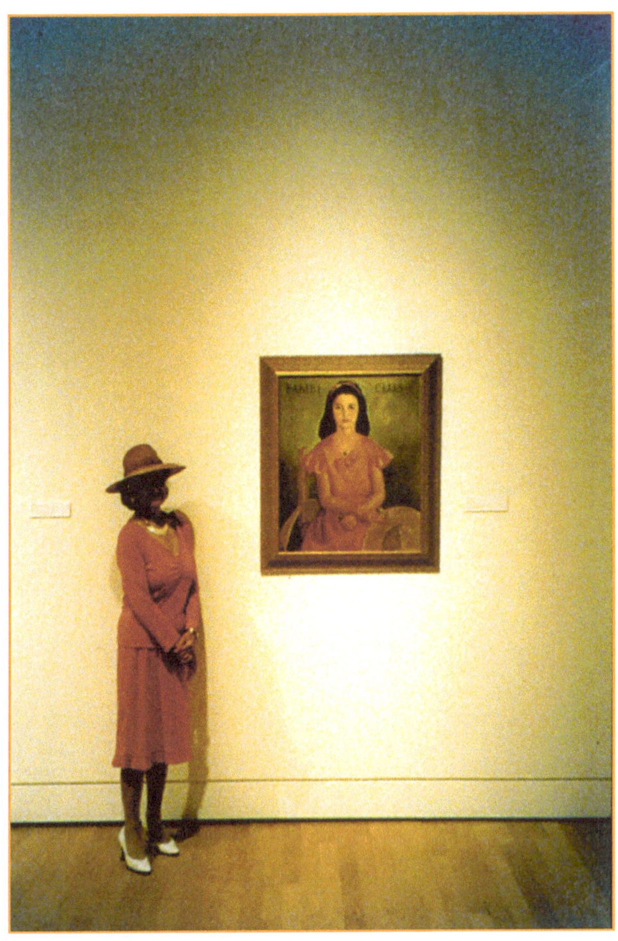

Bambi, the daughter of Fremont Ellis, stands beside the painting Tom Lea painted of her as a girl of twelve years old in 1933. He traded the painting to Ellis for land on the San Sebastian Ranch north of Santa Fe. It is an oil on canvas, 34 x 30 inches, framed. Accession no. 1989.3.1. It was a gift to the museum from Bambi Ellis in honor and admiration of Tom Lea. Photograph courtesy of the El Paso Museum of Art, El Paso, Texas.

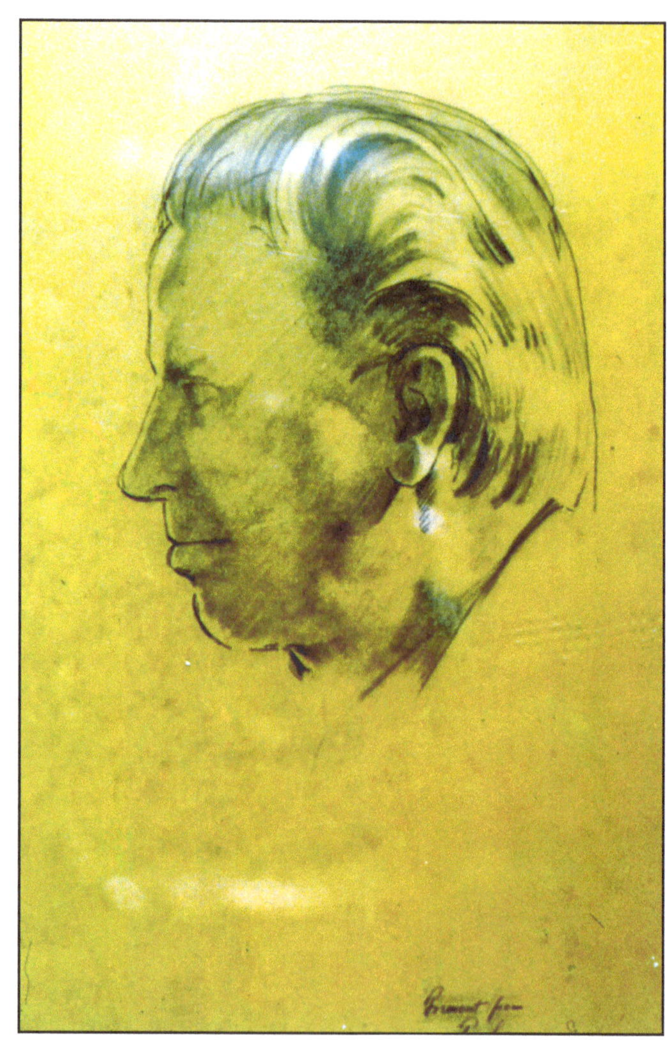

Drawing of Fremont F. Ellis by Tom Lea. Ellis considered him a dear close friend. Photograph courtesy of Bambi Ellis.

ACKNOWLEDGMENTS

Our sincere appreciation to the following persons and entities for their help in compiling this biography of Fremont F. Ellis:

American Artist Magazine for its cooperation in giving permission to use some of the material in articles it published about Fremont Ellis.

Stark Museum of Art in Orange, Texas, El Paso Museum of Art in El Paso, Texas, and Museum of Fine Arts, in Santa Fe, New Mexico, for their help and cooperation in providing slides of the Ellis Art Collections contained in their museums.

Tom Lea for his interesting, insightful, and loving introduction of this biography.

Fred Ellis for his help and support of this project.

Bernard Ewell, art appraiser, for his friendship and help throughout the years in all phases of Fremont Ellis' art business.

St. Francis Hotel in Santa Fe, New Mexico, for use of their painting, *Gathering Storm*, by Fremont Ellis.

Susan Ames, Frances Autry Teleki, and Sharon Foster for their help, support, and encouragement.

INTRODUCTION

by

Bambi Elizabeth Ellis

"Look at that gorgeous sunset," my friend murmured as we drove slowly along the Old Pecos Trail Road in Santa Fe. Without a word, I turned at the next crossroad and headed north to higher terrain. I went a short distance and pulled off into a parking area. From this location, we could see the brightly colored sunset streaking across the Jemez mountains to the west. Both of us sat in awed silence as we studied the vibrant pinks and oranges that decorated the skyline in dramatic changing colors and shapes.

Finally, I said, "Dad and I used to come up here to look at the sunsets. He would have loved this one. Look at those formations in the middle. They look like mythical animal shapes desperately leaping from the tongues of fire." I was aware of the awe and nostalgia and sadness in my voice. The days when my father and I sat in this very spot and enjoyed the New Mexico sunsets were gone forever now.

My friend said nothing, probably sensing the lonely feelings this sunset aroused in me. We watched a few more minutes while the brazen orange and red shades softened to hot pinks and then soft rose and lavender hues, and the subtle figures melted into the azure sky. I started my car and put it in reverse to turn around and go back to the Old Pecos Trail Road. "Only Dad could have painted that sunset," I said with a break in my voice.

Yes, my dad, Fremont Ellis, famed Southwestern painter, could have done justice to that glorious picture Mother Nature painted for us and allowed us to enjoy for a few short minutes. Dad would have looked at it, imprinted the colors and shapes on his memory, and then gone home and reproduced it in perfect detail so its beauty would have been preserved for all eternity. What a loss to everyone that he's gone, I thought sorrowfully.

My thoughts went on as I drove in silence. How I miss him, I mused. He had been so much a part of my life for all of my life. He was my hero when I was a little girl. He could make everything right for me. He was still my hero when I grew older and became interested in boys and young men. When those times in my life never worked out right, I always came back to him. He was my everlasting rock. It was inevitable that we would form the perfect working team. He painted the pictures; I marketed them. He hated the business end of his art career, and he entrusted the distribution of his paintings solely to me, secure in the feeling I would take care of his interests well. We were more than just father and daughter. We were partners and two kindred souls who understood and beautifully complemented each other.

He has been gone over twenty years now. I had one more project to do for him. I would assist in writing his biography, telling the story of Fremont F. Ellis, Southwestern painter extraordinaire, as only I know that story.

—Bambi Ellis
April 25, 2006

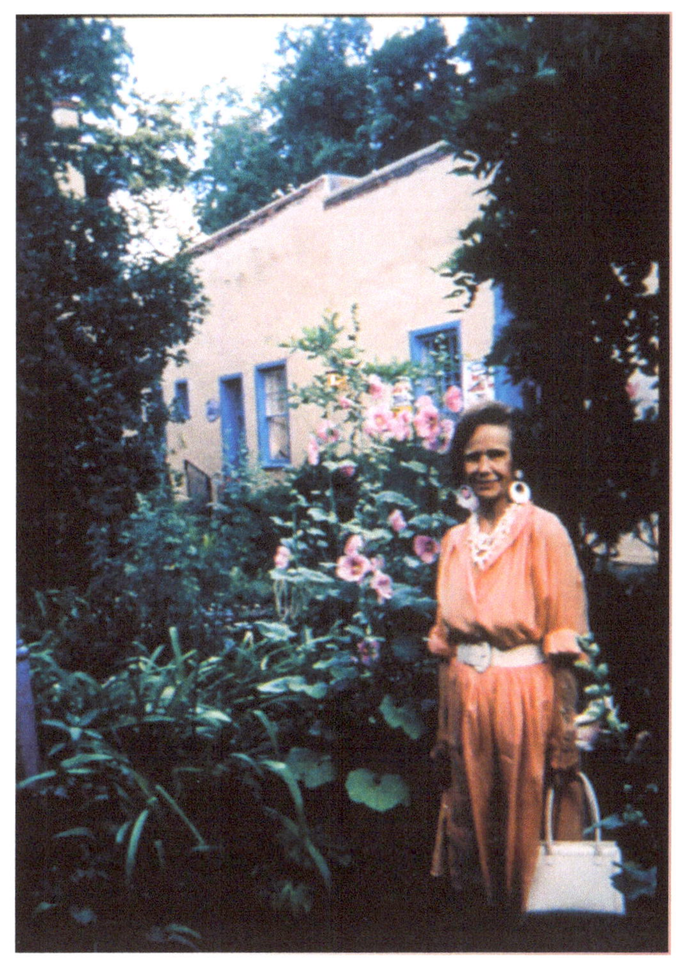

Bambi Ellis in 2009 in Santa Fe, New Mexico.
Photograph by Barbara Foster.

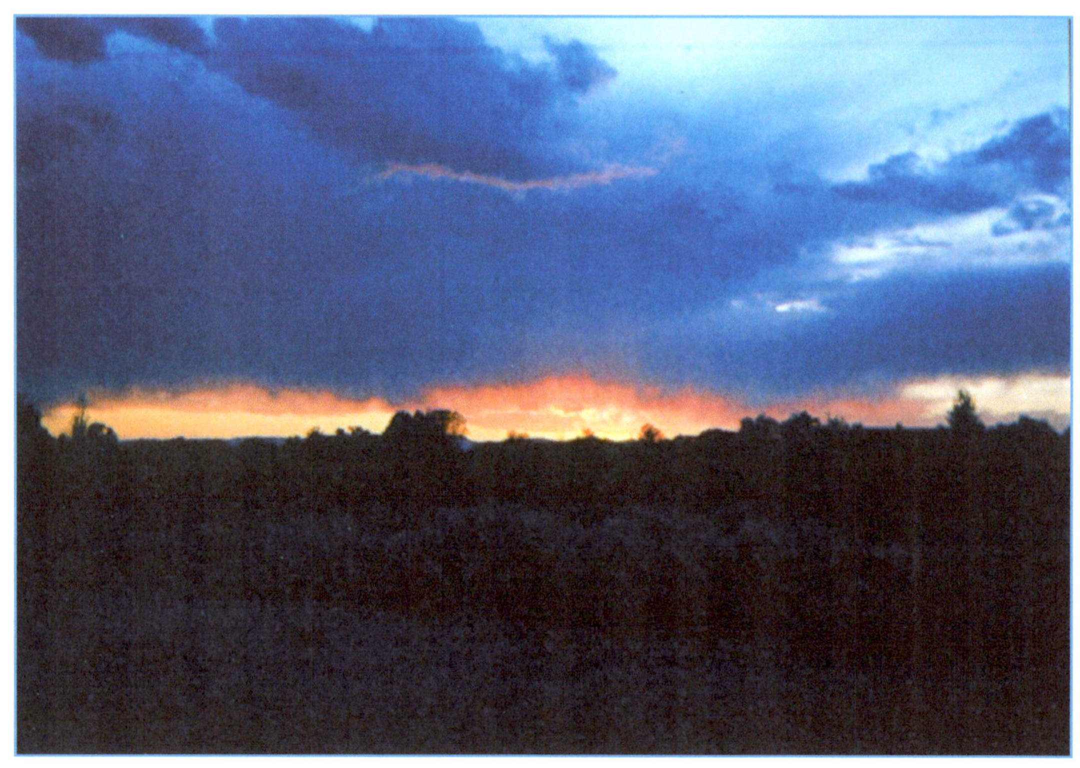

The sunset that inspired Ms. Ellis' introduction.
Photograph by Barbara Foster.

1

MONTANA BEGINNINGS

Fremont Ellis made his appearance into this world on October 2, 1897, in Virginia City, a remote Montana mining town. During the 1860s gold had been discovered, and now the area was again crowded with engineers and miners as it was experiencing another boom period. Having arrived by stage, his parents, Eleanor and Frederick Ellis, found the only available lodging in a two-room lumber building. The back room had been used by vigilantes as a make-shift morgue for the dead bodies of outlaws who were hung from the beam in the front room during the colorful history of the frontier town. Fremont was born under that historical beam.

In an article, "Art and Artists of New Mexico," that appeared in *New Mexico Magazine* in 1932, Ina Sizer Cassidy commented about the young artist, Fremont Ellis, who had chosen Santa Fe as his permanent home: "He was born in Virginia City, Montana, a town not often heard of these days, but from whose surrounding hills much of the gold was taken which went toward carrying on the Civil War. The hardihood required in this early life has remained with him and is shown in his work."

"I don't know if there was any influence in such a beginning, but I guess I got off to a roaring start," Ellis later commented about his birthplace. He was named for General John Fremont, a famous soldier and explorer of the West, who was greatly admired by his father. Subconsciously, he must have always known he must be tough like General Fremont in order to be a credit to his namesake and the western country they both loved.

At the time, Ellis' father was a dentist who traveled to sparsely populated areas throughout Montana, providing dental services and occasionally dabbling in some mining of his own. Shortly after his son was born, he moved his family to Pony, Montana. Pony was also a mining town set in the shadows of the mountain, Hollow Top, a volcanic peak towering up in the Beaverhead National Forest.

In addition to his dental work, Ellis' father also delved into the mining business. He usually didn't actually prospect for gold, but he staked the prospectors. If they found pay dirt, they shared it with him. He did work some claims in Pony, but the family stayed there only a few years.

Young Fremont had fond memories of the little mountain town. He remembered two Chinese women and was fascinated with the beautiful clothes they wore. They lived close to the Ellises, and he enjoyed visiting them and admiring their pretty dresses. He was intrigued with their tiny feet. He also retained a warm memory of a little girl who lived behind his house. One day when she had on a new dress, he took her by the hand and led her to his house and told his mother, "Look, isn't she pretty?" His eye for pretty colors and pretty girls started early in life, he later commented.

Perhaps this was the beginning of Fremont Ellis' appreciation for beauty. In an interview he later remarked, "Those kinds of things in your early life can really mean something, I think." He was probably influenced by the pleasing color and texture of those Chinese women's clothes and also by his memories of the beautiful mountain stream that ran near his home. The spectacular mountains that rose behind it may have been the reason for his later love for painting mountain landscapes.

In a few years, Frederick Ellis moved his family farther west to Missoula, Montana, and then on to Hamilton, Montana. Here he became acquainted with Marcus Daley, the millionaire copper king of Montana. Mining had paid off big for him in Butte. He had a large ranch in Hamilton where he bred and raised trotting horses. Fremont's father acquired one of Daley's horses and started training it to do complicated and amazing tricks. The horse, Don Felano, led him to a new career. He and Don Felano started playing fairs and carnivals and circuses, which led to vaudeville and then to motion pictures.

The Ellises stayed in Hamilton, Montana, long enough for Fremont to start and finish the first grade, and then they moved on. His father ran motion picture theatres in the West and the South, and he even made some motion pictures himself, producing the first movie about the Boy Scouts of America.

Fremont later remarked that his father was a man of imagination, great imagination with expertise in many areas. The family traveled all over the South and the West as dentistry was left behind and the theatrical business was pursued. Fremont was unable to attend public school because of all the traveling. He often said, "The only formal schooling I ever received was in Hamilton where I graduated from the first grade." After that his education consisted of teaching from his mother and father and "on the job learning."

Because of the nomadic existence of his family, Ellis never had a normal childhood in any way. They didn't stay in one place long enough for him to acquire many friends his own age, and he was surrounded almost exclusively by adults. As a result, his mother always said he grew up fast and developed a maturity beyond his years.

In recalling these early years, Fremont commented, "Except when I was very small, I was never young. I remember knowing about everything, even money, for I was always trying to get some."

Frederick Ellis instilled in his son a sense of responsibility, showmanship, and independence, as well as the adventurous wish to "see the other side of the mountain." His mother exposed him to the wonders of design, light, and color at an early age. Her interest stemmed from her work in designing hats. From the time he was a toddler, young Fremont loved to look at beautiful fabrics, textures, and interiors. As he grew, he became more fascinated by intricate designs such as those found in oriental rugs.

Even though Fremont Ellis had little formal education, he developed a lifelong hunger for learning, thanks to his parents' influence and their determination to develop in their precocious son an inner confidence and the belief that he could teach himself anything he put his mind to.

His parents realized that Fremont didn't have the patience to be cooped up in a classroom, probably because of the gypsy life style the family embraced. The final realization of this fact happened in South Carolina where they were at the time, and where they had decided to send twelve year old Fremont to a boarding school. After repeated escapes from the rigid and stiff environment of this respected house of learning, his father finally gave in and let him stay at home and accompany him and his mother wherever they traveled.

As the Ellis family traveled throughout Georgia, the Carolinas, and Virginia during his pre-teen years, young Fremont was exposed to the architecture and interiors of the old southern mansions. Many of these estates had been transformed into inns, and the family enjoyed staying in those charming places. Such beauty and magnificence made a vivid and lasting impression on young Fremont. He later had very definite ideas as to the decoration themes of his own homes.

The family traveled back to the Northeast, and Fremont's parents encouraged him to expand his interests to include cameras. By the age of thirteen, he was knowledgeable enough to earn a meager income by taking portraits at the county fairs and developing the pictures on the spot. Life had been rich and full for the young boy, and would only become more exciting as time went on.

2

A YOUNG BOY DISCOVERS the METROPOLITAN MUSEUM of ART

In the fall of 1910, after touring the United States for eight years, the Ellis family purchased a new automobile and went to New York City where Fremont's father and his horse had a booking with a well-known vaudeville show. Because he and the car didn't see eye-to-eye, the senior Ellis hired a chauffeur named George to drive them. George and Fremont became great friends during the trip.

Up to the age of twelve, Charles Russell, a Montana Western painter who had crossed paths with the Ellis family during their sojourn in that northwestern state, was the only artist Ellis had ever met. Frederick Ellis was intrigued with that artist's Western drawings and paintings as well as his engaging personality, but the family association with Russell was short and his influence on Fremont was probably minimal. But now, in New York City, young Fremont was about to be introduced to the world of art.

One morning Eleanor Ellis told her son she wanted him to go with her to the Metropolitan Museum of Art. He balked at the idea, but he didn't want to disappoint her, and he knew it was an opportunity to hang out with his friend, George, and that was the part of the outing that appealed to him. This was a decision that opened up an entirely new world and changed Fremont's life from that moment on.

When Fremont climbed the impressive steps leading to the entry of the museum and went inside, his eyes were immediately drawn to the glorious paintings, especially those of Albert Bierstadt. He later described his reaction to the paintings: "It was like turning on a light inside a dark house or as if you'd never been able to see and suddenly could. I looked at those paintings, and I couldn't believe my eyes. The first thing I was fascinated with was the look of the paint surface; then the next thing was the illusion of three-dimensional space on a flat surface; and then, it was the impression of light." He was particularly taken with the light effects and the warm romantic feel of the West in the Bierstadt works. Over the next few weeks, he returned to the Metropolitan again and again to study the paintings, arriving when the doors opened and leaving reluctantly when they were locked for the night. Bierstadt's influence stayed with him all his life.

He later said, "I was fascinated as I looked at the depths and the light effects. I couldn't figure out how it could happen." Ellis decided to acquire some watercolors and try to capture what he saw portrayed on the various gallery walls.

At that time it was common for young student artists to set up their easels in the galleries and copy the paintings. But Fremont was shy and didn't want to show his inexperience by painting in the company of the other artists, so he chose to purchase sepia or black and white prints of his favorite paintings which were on sale at the museum and take them home where at night he would practice his painting in the privacy of his own studio in his apartment. Using the print reproduction as a guide, the budding artist would study the subject's shapes and use charcoal to block them out on his canvas, all the while struggling with his draftsmanship. Then he would return to the museum to memorize the colors in the painting and rush home and attempt to duplicate from memory the colors he saw.

In retrospect, Fremont's shyness and reluctance to paint in public worked to his advantage. It forced him to develop an extraordinary visual memory, and a keen sense of color and light, leading to his unique talent for translating the images in his mind's eye onto the canvas.

In a July, 1975, in an interview with Barbara Whipple, a free-lance writer for the *American Artist Magazine,* Ellis recalled: "I think that was the beginning of my memory training. I've learned to get a quick, overall look at a subject. I don't examine it too closely, and I guess that's the reason I'm the kind of dabbler I am. I don't delineate the painting too much. When you look at something, it's apparent that in your mind you bring something to it as well as what's there. I've come to the conclusion that if you don't bring anything to it, you're not going to get anything out of it."

He went on to elaborate: "I paint this way even today. If I see something outdoors that strikes me, and if I have the time and the weather is such that I can set up my easel and paint out there, I do. But I don't face the subject. I want to paint what is in my mind, which is the first thing I saw. That's not out there; it's only partially out there. If you start to look at the subject out there, pretty soon the subject will dominate you. You'll be doing what's there, whether it fits what's here (he tapped his head) in your mind or not. Physical vision you must have, but you must have the mental vision to go with it. You see with the mental vision as well as the physical."

Fremont soon determined that he needed oil paints as a medium since watercolors only offered so much. The effect he was trying to reproduce could only be achieved with oils. As the end of 1910 drew near, his parents asked what he wanted for Christmas. He knew his heart's desire would be expensive, but nothing else would do, and his parents managed, even though money was scarce, to place a box of oil paints under the Christmas tree for his special present.

Elated, young Fremont began an extraordinary period of teaching himself how to paint. He continued his "method" of using a black and white "reproduction" as a guide to outline the basic shapes in the painting and then return once again to the museum to study the original for its treatment of light and color, rushing back to the apartment to fill in the shapes, using his keen memory.

One day when he was particularly pleased with his painting, he held it up for his mother to evaluate. "What do you think?" he asked. "What is my painting worth, Mother?"

Eleanor Ellis looked at the strong dabs of paint and the simulation of one of Bierstadt's famous paintings and wrinkled her forehead in thought. "I think this painting is worth uncountable riches because it is starting you on a career that will startle the art world. This painting is worth more than you can ever imagine."

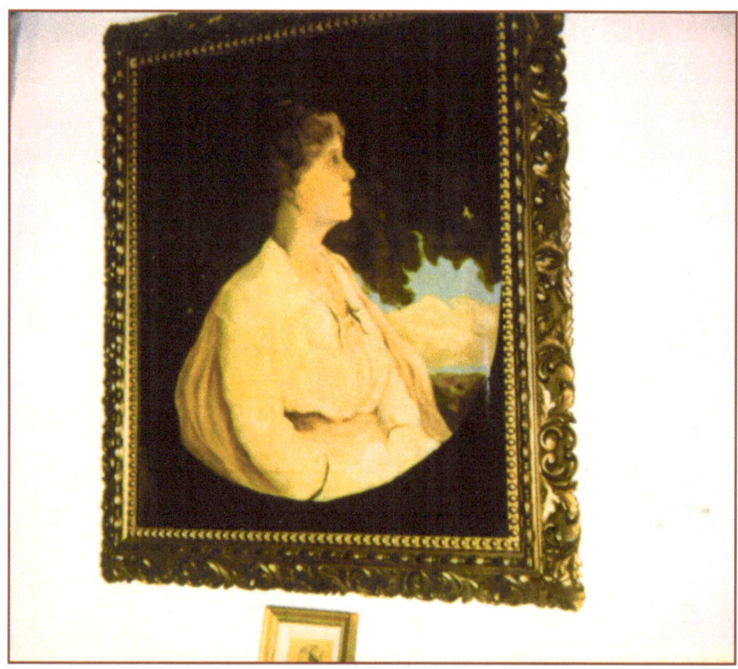

Fremont F. Ellis painted this picture of his mother when he was sixteen years old.
Photograph courtesy of Fred Ellis.

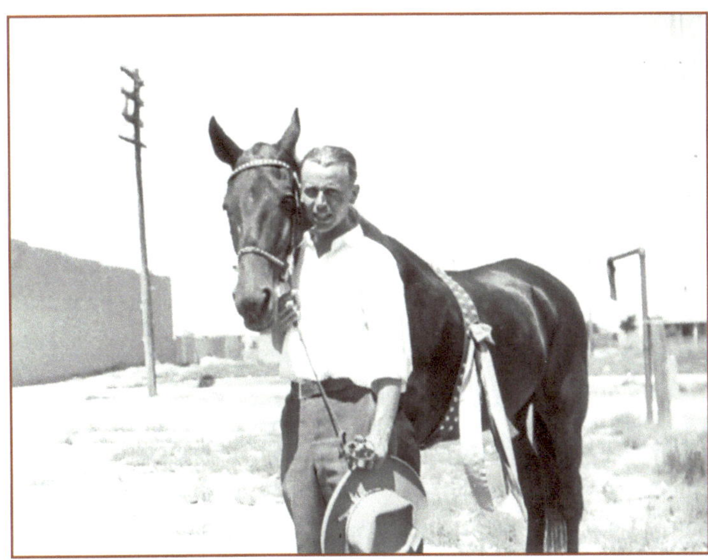

Fremont F. Ellis with his father's famous show horse, Don Felano. Photograph courtesy of Bambi Ellis.

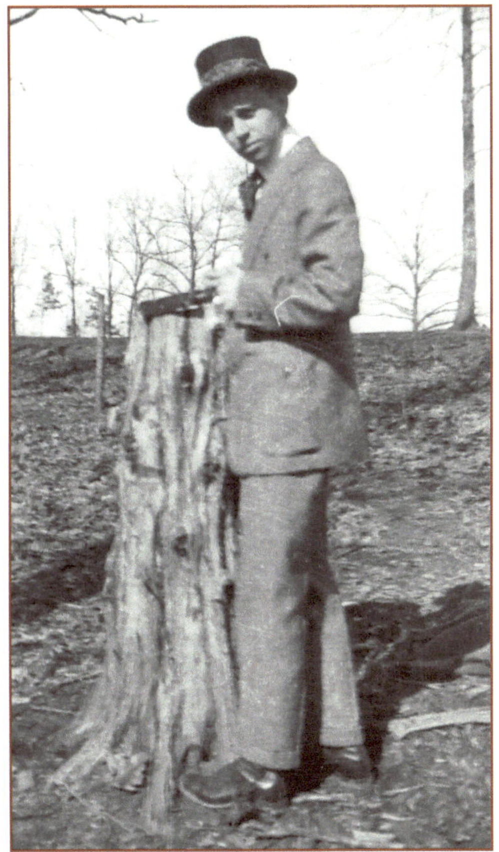

Fremont F. Ellis as a young boy in New York City. Photograph courtesy of Bambi Ellis.

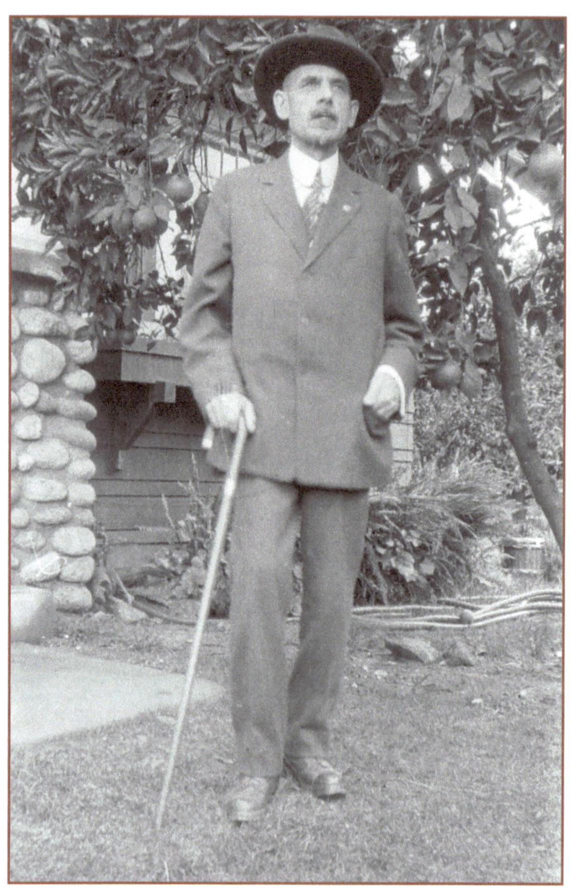

Fremont F. Ellis' father, Frederick Ellis.
Photograph courtesy of Bambi Ellis.

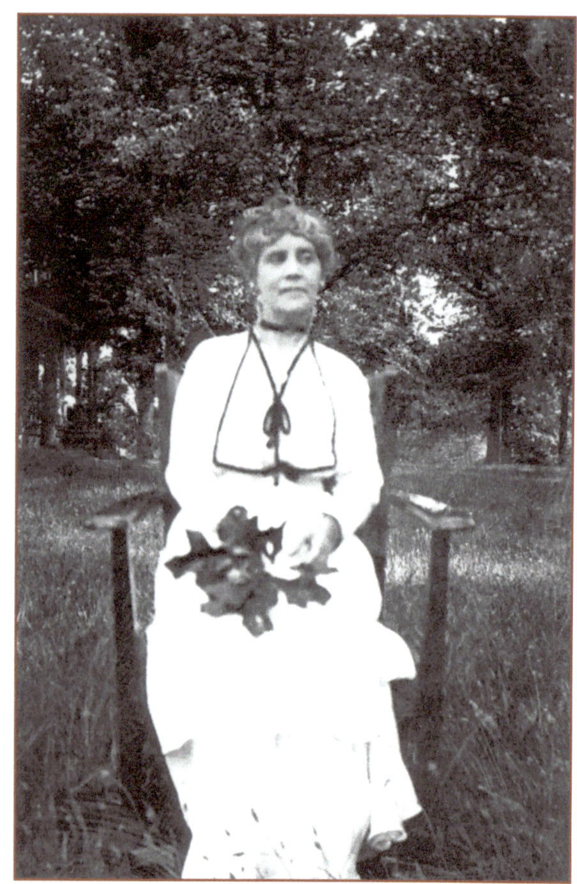

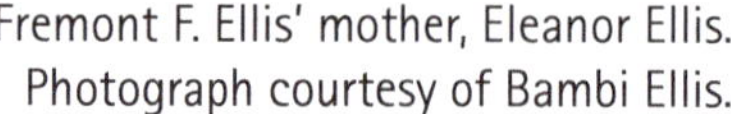

Fremont F. Ellis' mother, Eleanor Ellis.
Photograph courtesy of Bambi Ellis.

3

AN ARTIST EVOLVES

While in New York City after his many trips to the Metropolitan Museum, Fremont attended the National Academy's annual exhibit of paintings. Here he had an experience similar to the one in the Metropolitan. But the colors in these paintings were taken from nature and the American Impressionists were his models for painting from that point on. He began reading everything he could get his hands on about art and artists, with a special focus on landscape painting. He especially enjoyed reading biographies to gain insights into how and why others became artists.

When asked in later years if he was ever tempted to study under any of the impressionistic artists whose work he admired, he stated, "No, no. There, you see, I have a peculiar quirk there. I don't know why I have it. As I said, I never liked to go to school, any kind of school. But even though I never liked to go to school, I am studying. I am quite a reader. I read all the time. I've been studying all my life, and still am."

Fremont's father talked him into enrolling in the Art Student's League when he was about fourteen years old. The school accepted him after seeing some of his paintings even though he was the youngest student they had. He enjoyed the classes more than he thought he would, but he stayed there only about three months. He wanted to be free to travel with his parents, and he felt the outdoors was his best classroom.

By now he had expanded his horizons and had begun painting outdoors where he could interact directly with the values and tones of the colors and light before him. This was a major change from his previous experience with the old masters at the Metropolitan.

Fremont told Barbara Whipple in an interview for *American Artist Magazine* later in his painting career: "I particularly remember a day when I took my paints up along the Hudson River, and I saw two very accomplished artists painting there, and I stayed in the background and just watched them. Instead of drawing and coloring it in, I saw them taking the paint and putting brush strokes side by side and evolving the image that was there with the paint. This seemed like a great idea to me." Up until then the boy artist had always made a drawing of his intended creation and filled it in, and he always had problems with his draftsmanship.

The next day he returned to the same spot and attempted to copy this new technique. It worked, and he was delighted with the result. It pointed him in a new direction and elevated his painting to a new level.

At the age of fifteen, while the family was living in Salem, North Carolina, Fremont took pleasure in assisting his father who had gone into managing movie houses and was also attempting to make movies himself in his spare time. Fremont's responsibility in the movie house business was to make sure the film got to the late train each night to be shipped on to the next movie house. He also, along with Fremont's half-sister, provided background music for the silent films as they were shown. She played the piano and he played the drums. Afterward, he would scurry back to his studio to paint into the early hours of the morning.

After traveling through Virginia and painting in the Tennessee mountains, Fremont reconnected with his parents in El Paso, Texas, where they had settled due to his father's need to be in a dry climate for health reasons.

4

El PASO, OPTOMETRY and ART

Shortly after their move to El Paso, Fremont Ellis' father became ill and Eleanor, his mother, decided Fremont should learn another skill to help with the family income. At the suggestion of an uncle, he went to Los Angeles for a nine month optometry course, but after eight months he left because he felt he had learned enough about refractions to make prescription glasses. He returned to El Paso to be near his parents, and he set up an optometry practice, all the while continuing to paint every day.

Due in large part to his honesty and integrity, Fremont's business failed shortly after it opened. He explained to his parents that he didn't prescribe glasses for people he felt didn't need them, therefore his income was meager. Nevertheless, he made many friends, and because of his expertise with refractions, another successful optometrist and former competitor eagerly hired him. Life was working out for him. He was up every morning at dawn working on landscapes and was able to paint for some time before he went to work at eight. He was earning enough to be able to help his parents financially as well as continue his painting.

Finally Fremont's father's health improved. Always the natural promoter, he felt an exhibit of Fremont's work was necessary to make El Pasoans aware of his capability and talent, so he made arrangements with a local University Club for a showing. Fremont protested on the grounds that he lacked enough good work to present to the public, but his father persuaded his reluctant son, telling him that the time was ripe for him to be given public recognition as a professional artist.

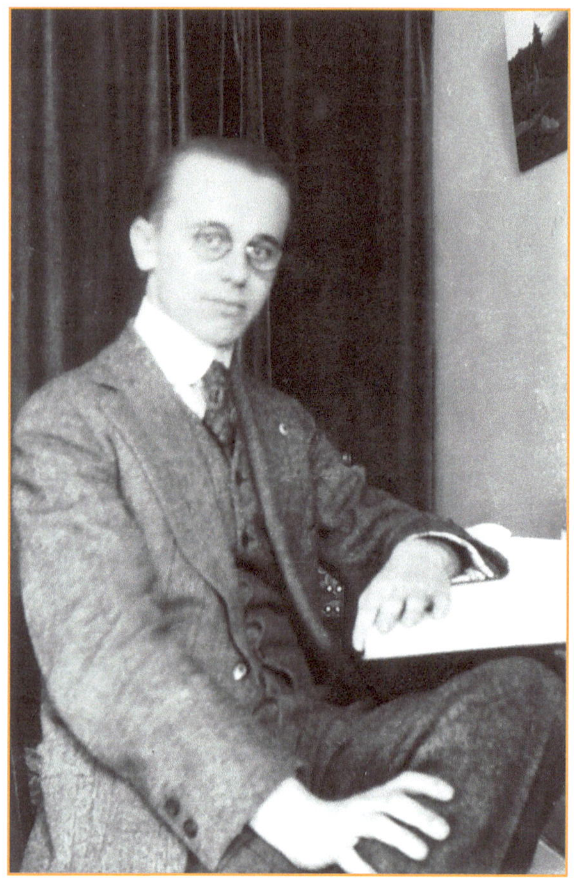

Fremont F. Ellis, eighteen years old and a young optometrist. Photograph courtesy of Bambi Ellis.

In January, 1919, the modest artist exhibited some thirty paintings of Southwest landscapes at the University Club in El Paso, his first formal one man show. As reported by an article appearing in a local paper, it was a great success. Critics wrote, "Ellis has caught and fixed on canvas the very spirit, soul, and poetry of the desert." His works sold so well that a dealer in El Paso agreed to represent Fremont Ellis and his paintings and additionally arranged with the Vose Gallery in Boston to handle the young artist's work. Both the dealer and his father, along with his boss at the time, then persuaded the young man to give up optometry and become a full time painter. After all, he was getting as much as one hundred fifty dollars for each of his paintings. That was a handsome price in those days.

Ellis told an art patron who was surprised and excited to find an artist of his talents in El Paso: "Art is art, whether it be in Paris, London, New York, or El Paso. I feel a good artist paints what he feels more often than what he sees." The style and philosophy of impressionistic painting was becoming obvious in the emotion he was able to portray in his paintings.

The El Paso Morning Times in an article written by Frank Wittram on December 15, 1918, reported remarks made by A. Montgomery, the "farmer painter," widely known throughout the United States and Europe in art circles because of his paintings of corn, sheep, and chickens. Montgomery stated: "The people in El Paso don't need my corn and sheep and chickens, but they do need to surrender themselves with the evidence of art in our midst. If El Paso doesn't wake up and claim Fremont Ellis, a great painter of the desert, the sun, and the sky, I'll take a hand and make a great man out of him by placing him where he belongs." This was a tribute from one of the best known and most famous of American artists at that time.

The editor of *The El Paso Morning Times* wrote of Fremont Ellis in 1919: "He delights in indulging in a riot of melting colors, all blending in exquisite harmony and glowing in subtle lights and shade, so characteristic of the far-flung reaches of the arid plain. His paintings remind me of one of Longfellow's lines, 'Torrents of light and river of air' or, as a stellar highway where the billowing clouds race in aerial sport...."

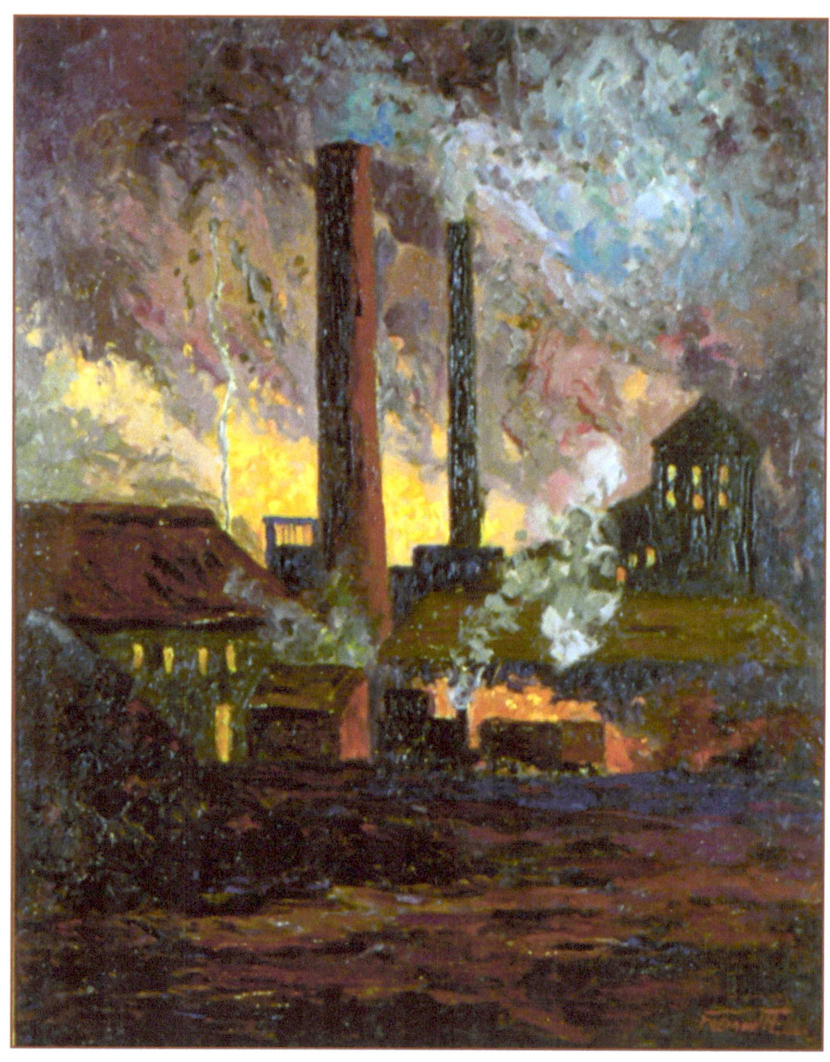

El Paso Smelter at Night, 1919, oil on canvas, 36 x 30 1/8 inches.
Courtesy of the El Paso Museum of Art Collection, El Paso, Texas. Accession no. 1971, 5.1.
The painting was a gift of the artist to the museum.

5

SANTA FE, ENCHANTED VILLAGE

With his father's ability to attract interesting people and introduce them to his family, Fremont had the good fortune to become acquainted with Albert Severs and his wife, a musical couple who had moved to Santa Fe, New Mexico, to establish a music school. Having heard them rave about this ancient town, a restless twenty-one year old Fremont decided to travel to Santa Fe in June of 1918 to visit his friends and spend the summer.

The Severs met him at the Santa Fe Railroad Depot, and Fremont never forgot his first impression of Santa Fe as they walked up San Francisco Street toward the Plaza. He marveled at the limitless blue sky, the puffy dramatic clouds billowing up over the northern mountains, the golden sun on the cottonwoods, and the creative atmosphere that surrounded him. Santa Fe permeated deeply into his searching soul. His comments later were, "It was the most beautiful place I'd ever seen. Even though I had traveled all over the United States, I'd never seen anything like this unique place for pure and unspoiled beauty. I gazed at the adobe houses with windows that gleamed as though they had been polished and the geraniums sitting brightly in the windows. There were burros on the streets and poplar trees along the road. It was heaven." What started as a summer vacation turned into a burning desire to make Santa Fe his permanent home.

From that first day, Fremont Ellis was intrigued with the landscape, the architecture, and the atmosphere of Santa Fe, but that was not everything that delighted him in this historic city. One afternoon while enjoying a dish of ice cream in The Confectionery, he had met Laurencita Gonzales, a beautiful young girl who was a direct descendent of one of the Spanish colonists who had settled the area. Her charming manner and striking appearance so fascinated him that he began to spend more time at The Confectionery, eating ice cream that "Lencha," as he now called her, served him. He was trying to work up enough courage to ask Mrs. Gonzales for permission to visit her daughter.

Lencha's mother was not thrilled to learn that a *Gringo* wished to pay court to her daughter. Only grudgingly did she permit Fremont to come by for a cup of chocolate and make small talk with them while Lencha sat with her eyes downcast, being careful not to betray her true interest in their visitor.

Eventually, Lencha's mother accepted Fremont as a decent and kind man and even looked forward to his frequent visits. Nevertheless, it was made clear that any thought of marriage between the young couple was impossible because Lencha was expected to marry someone of her own faith. The teachings of Catholicism the family had devoutly followed in Spain and continued to prioritize faithfully in this adopted land were not to be ignored. However, Fremont was undeterred by the mother's concerns, and he promised his Lencha that he would find a way for them to be married.

Soon after, he returned to El Paso for a visit with his parents. They were both delighted by his announcement that he had found the girl he wanted to marry in Santa Fe, and he intended to return to make her his bride as soon as possible. He also shared his plans to give himself five years in Santa Fe to hone his craft, learn new techniques, paint the wondrous surroundings, and, hopefully, become the caliber of painter he admired and respected in other skilled artists.

Thus, armed with this two-fold purpose, Fremont returned to Santa Fe where he convinced Lencha they should be married in April, 1920, by a Justice of the Peace. They headed for Taos as a group of artists there had invited Fremont to join them. They stopped off in Espanola to visit Bernie Romero, the cousin who had stood up with Lencha at her wedding. They were so happy there that Lencha persuaded Fremont to rent a small adobe house on the banks of the Rio Grande River where they honeymooned. They took hikes along the river and in the surrounding hills, and Fremont sketched the scenes made even more beautiful to him by his love for his new bride. The newlyweds lived on beans from that area and apples picked from a nearby orchard until Fremont was able to convince a man at a local mercantile store to trade food for some of his sketches.

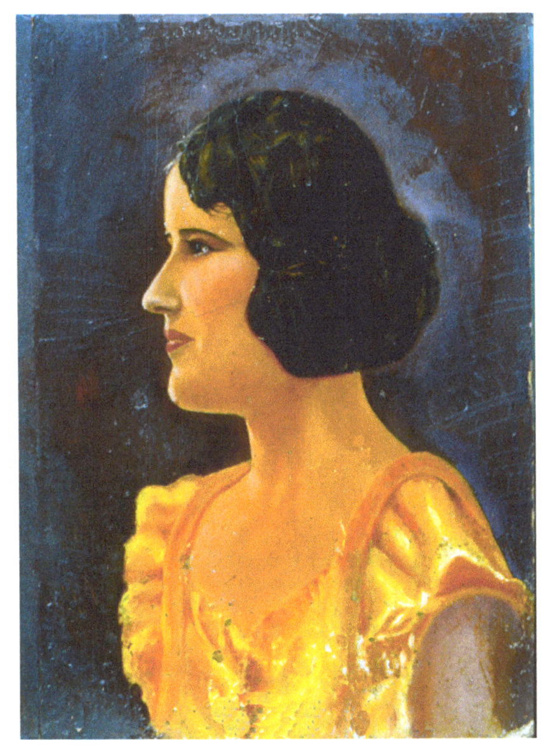

Portrait of his young wife, Laurencita Gonzales de Ellis. Photograph courtesy of Bambi Ellis.

It was a time of love and discovery for the young couple. Fremont spoke only a smattering of Spanish, and his bride was no more fluent in English. But their determination to be together was all the motivation they needed for learning their respective languages. They understood the language of love perfectly, and it inspired them to work for proficiency in Spanish and English.

Meanwhile, Lencha's mother was determined that the young couple would have their marriage sanctified in the church. With the cathedral in Santa Fe as the setting, Fremont and Lencha agreed to be married a second time a month later before a priest, thus satisfying the Gonzales family. The young couple stayed in Santa Fe to make their permanent home, and Lencha's mother was pleased to have her daughter near her again.

Fremont was for the most part content with his life now. He embraced the responsibilities of his union with Lencha, he had good friends in the area, he now had the opportunity to study the techniques of top artists, and he could even have an exhibit of his own work at the Fine Arts Museum on the Plaza. But, in spite of Santa Fe being an ideal place to live and paint and study, Fremont discovered after a time that it was not yet a lucrative place for selling one's paintings.

The elder Ellises had now moved to Los Angeles, and ever feeling the need to be close to his parents both physically and emotionally, Fremont and Lencha decided to move west in the hope of finding a better market for his artwork. They moved into a studio, and Fremont tried to concentrate on his painting.

During this period, Lencha became well acquainted with her husband's parents. They were both from England even though they had met in New York City. At that time Eleanor had her own millenary shop where she designed and created hats, and Fred Ellis had spotted her through the window of the shop one day as he walked down Fifth Avenue. The courtship was short and in the decisive way Fred Ellis did everything, he made the pretty English lady his wife shortly thereafter. It was a second marriage for both, and Fremont was their only child although each had children from their first marriages.

Fred and Eleanor Ellis were different from the average American couple because of their unique interests. They loved the Bohemian life style, and traveled and lived in many places in the United States before settling in El Paso. They adored Fremont and made him part of their lives and work no matter which project Fred Ellis was currently pursuing. At the same time, they allowed him the freedom to pursue his own interests. Certainly they had always encouraged his painting. They had faith in his artistic ability. The same was true with their approval of the wife he had chosen. They respected his judgment and feelings for the beautiful Spanish girl even though they couldn't communicate with her very well. They loved Lencha and wholeheartedly accepted her into their family.

6

ADVENTURES with HARPER HENRY and *The Ford of Art*

Even in Los Angeles, times were lean for the young artist. While he continued to paint on a daily basis, he still had trouble finding a market for his work. Deeply depressed one day, Ellis left his studio for a walk downtown. He had decided to quit painting forever when he unexpectedly ran into his father who had been looking for him.

"I just sent a model up to your place for you to paint," he told his son.

Fremont replied in a despondent voice, "A model! What did you do that for? If it was Jesus Christ himself, I wouldn't paint him."

"Well," laughed his father. "you'd just better turn around and go back there because this man is as close to Jesus Christ as you'll ever get!"

Upon returning to his studio, Ellis was introduced to Harper Henry, a kindly, barefoot, bearded man dressed in white from head to toe. He was a Renaissance man, possessing many talents as an engineer, designer, mechanic, and promoter, all in one strange looking package. He was fascinated by Fremont's creativity and style of painting, especially his treatment of light. The two of them immediately found a kindred spirit in each other and touched on many subjects, not only art. Thus began a long and remarkable friendship between Fremont Ellis, Harper Henry, and their young wives.

The world owes a debt of gratitude to Harper Henry, for he was a welcome relief for Fremont and a much needed tonic for this low period in his creative life.

Inspired by Henry's enthusiasm and entrepreneurial spirit, he decided to continue painting.

Henry was a wizard at mechanical things and could build almost anything. Inspired by his friendship with Fremont, he conceived the idea for a vehicle they would call The Ford of Art. It was designed as a customized self-contained unit on a Ford Model-T chassis. It would have seats as well as sleeping quarters for them and their wives. It would also have its own water supply and other comforts. Once built, all four planned to hop into the vehicle and journey to the south rim of the Grand Canyon.

To accomplish this dream, Henry invited the young Ellises to move to a little house on his father's place in the San Fernando Valley called Freedom Hill. There they would build The Ford of Art while Fremont would also concentrate on his painting. Freedom Hill was an isolated piece of land Henry's father had purchased as a place where people "could be themselves."

On his first day there, Fremont headed for the workshop to help Henry with the car. He soon encountered other residents who, he noticed, were wearing no clothes and seemed totally unconcerned about the fact. Now he knew why the place was named Freedom Hill. It was a nudist colony.

For several months Henry, with occasional help from Ellis, worked on the car which evolved into a unique custom job, years ahead of any manufactured cars of the time. Airplane fabric covered the hardwood frame on the outside; on the inside it was lined with a mahogany veneer. Best of all, Henry designed the interior space to include a miniature gallery for Fremont to display his paintings. Their plan was to sell the art work along the way to defray expenses.

To complete the preparations, Henry wrote and printed a promotional brochure about Fremont Ellis and his art to give out to people they'd meet on their journey. In addition, he designed and constructed a special box for Fremont's oil paints. They were now ready to begin their trek to the Grand Canyon.

In the 1920s the road east from Los Angeles to the Grand Canyon was little more than an unpaved path through the desert, dotted occasionally with a sign from the AAA. Henry did all the driving, barely averaging fifteen miles per hour. In spite of mechanical breakdowns, and a dearth of water and gasoline, Henry calmly solved all problems and kept the party in good spirits. He entertained everyone with philosophical discourse on the nutrient value of yogurt to such complex ideas as nuclear theory and the ultimate development of the atomic bomb. Ellis always admired him as a genius.

After nearly a month of long hot days of driving, they arrived at their destination and Ellis put his paintings on display at a hotel on the south rim of the Grand Canyon. They immediately attracted great interest. At the end of four days, the travelers had made some respectable sales and Fremont, who was generous with money when he had it, suggested they all celebrate and eat a good dinner. They had been living on the health food the Henrys had brought along, but that night they enjoyed steaks and crab and lobster along with desserts. But the next day they were sick from all the rich foods. Fremont remarked, "What a shame. All that money spent just to make ourselves sick."

7

BACK to the CITY DIFFERENT

From the Grand Canyon, the party traveled east and north to Santa Fe. It was now the summer of 1921. The Henrys returned to Los Angeles, but Fremont and Lencha decided to stay in Santa Fe. Having made a mark as an artist during his previous stay there, Fremont was welcomed back by his fellow artists and introduced to others who had arrived while he had been on the West Coast.

To support Lencha and himself, Fremont went to work for a local photographer, using his expertise in the darkroom to develop pictures. It was an ideal job because he could devote his evening hours to developing film while reserving a good part of the day for painting. He had given himself another five year deadline to improve on his already distinctive painting style.

8

Los Cinco Pintores, "The FIVE NUTS in the ADOBE HUTS"

In the fall of 1921, Fremont Ellis and four other artists in Santa Fe, Jozef Bakos, Walter Mruk, Willard Nash, and Will Shuster, having found that they all shared a common philosophy, banded together to form the community's first organized artist group. So was born *Los Cinco Pintores* (The Five Painters).

As they were initially discussing the neame for the group, Fremont said, "Why not just plain and simply, The Five Painters?"

But Lencha objected, "Oh no, that's too simple. Call yourselves *Los Cinco Pintores.* That's got a ring to it."

All five painters agreed and the name stuck.

At the time, all five artists were under thirty years of age, and each had migrated from different parts of the country. While each had his own individual style of expression, as a whole they represented a new generation of young and enthusiastic painters caught up in the spirit of the 1920s. They all shared the determination to make a living at what they enjoyed and knew best—painting.

As a result of their innovation and camaraderie, *Los Cinco Pintores* became one of the most important and well known artist groups in the Southwest, and is remembered as the seed that spawned the now famous artists' row up Canyon Road in Santa Fe.

Unlike the well-established and influential *Taos Society of Arts,* which had certain limited criteria for membership, *Los Cinco Pintores* was loosely organized, which was exactly the way they planned it and wanted the organization to be. Their founding principle was simple. They would meet, sketch, paint, and exhibit together for their own enjoyment and achievement while each would maintain his unique style, technique and manner of expression. By having a group identity, they were convinced they could draw greater public attention to themselves and their work rather than working individually. To signify their membership in *Los Cinco Pintores*, they designed a five pointed symbol which they integrated into each if their signatures on their paintings.

November 1, 1921, marked the first of several exhibitions of *Los Cinco Pintores* at the Armory in Santa Fe. These young painters pledged to take art to the people and not to surrender to commercialism.

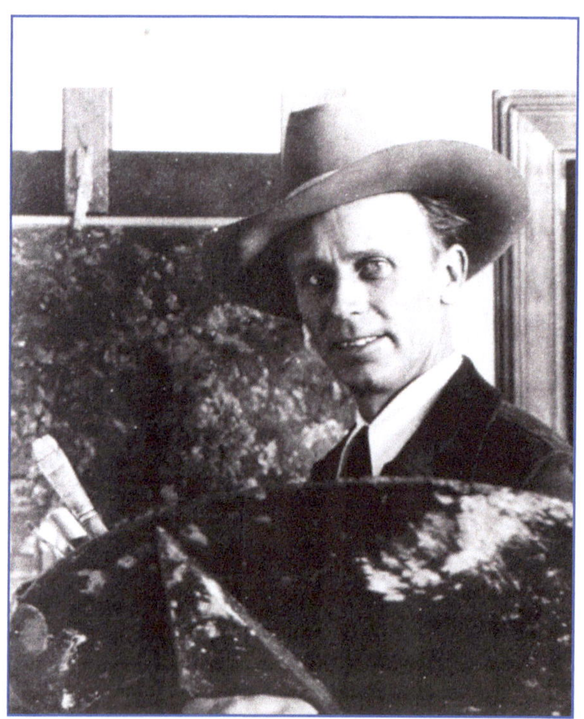

Fremont Ellis as a young painter and a member of *Los Cinco Pintores.* Photograph courtesy of Bambi Ellis.

At about the same time that *Los Cinco Pintores* was formed, Frank Applegate entered the picture. He owned land up the canyon on El Camino Del Monte Sol and offered to sell each artist a portion of this property on credit. Moreover, he would give each of them seven hundred dollars for materials so they could build their own houses.

Of the five, Josef Bakos was the only one who knew anything about building a house. He was a trained carpenter and an expert builder, especially with adobe bricks. He patiently shared his expertise with the other four, showing them how to dig foundations, make adobe bricks, fit doors and windows, and construct fireplaces. They toiled for three full months, making many mistakes along the way.

One major misstep was building their adobe houses in the wrong season of the year. They started in October when there was no summer sun to properly cure the bricks. It was a miracle that any of the structures stood up for any length of time after they were constructed. But through all the difficulties, the houses were finished and finally, on a cold day in 1921, Ellis and Lencha moved into their humble home. Despite its flaws, it was a proud moment for Fremont. What an accomplishment, building his own home!

Fremont later related in an interview with Robert Sanchez his frustrations in building his first home. He said, "I didn't know anything about building. I'd worked a little for Nordfeldt, making furniture. But Bakos was the cabinet maker; he knew his stuff. Shus (Will Shuster), too. I was the dumbest.

"Like all *Gringos,* I thought I was smarter than those two guys working for me. I told them to mix the mud; I'd lay the adobes. The first row I sailed right along. I put the second row right over it, adobe for adobe. I was starting the third the same way when one of these guys apologetically suggested that I alternate bricks, using a half adobe at the beginning of every other row. I decided he could do it. I'd mix mud.

"In spite of the wavy walls that we built, the house stood up with its four walls. We put the roof on it and ran some water from a hose on top of the house to see if it leaked. It did. I had to give up and hire a professional roofer to put the roof on the house.

"That house was quite a challenge," Ellis concluded. "But we enjoyed that little home very much for ten years."

Happy in their modest dwellings and devoted to their painting, *Los Cinco Pintores* enjoyed nightly social gatherings to offset their serious daytime efforts to create masterpieces. They also developed a reputation for being impulsive, which at times got them into trouble. The local townspeople often shook their heads and muttered regarding some of the members' latest antics, "But what can you expect from one of the five nuts in the five mud huts?" They also developed a reputation for being incorrigible pleasure seekers.

The Santa Fe Armory soon offered the five artists space in their building to exhibit their work. People started coming to their exhibits and, in fact, they began to receive more interest than the older, more established artists in the area. Later, in 1921, the Fine Arts Museum allowed them to exhibit there. They were the first artists to exhibit in the newly constructed museum which had been designed and built by Carlos Vierra, a fellow friend, artist, and architect.

9

The FREMONT ELLIS FAMILY Fights for Survival and Recognition

On May 13, 1922, Fremont and Lencha's daughter, Bambi, arrived on the scene. The next year both of Fremont's parents died just months apart. This marked the beginning of a depressing and anxious period in his life. Even though his paintings were being recognized, he was still finding that there was only a small market for his work in Santa Fe. Adding to the burden was his realization that he had little business savvy, typical of many creative geniuses. Again he was discouraged and felt alone and poor, partially caused by the loss of both parents. His little girl, Bambi, may have been the sole reason he did not totally give in to his deep despair.

Always a problem solver, Lencha suggested they could cut back on expenses if they were to rent out their home on Camino del Monte Sol and move into a little adobe house on De Vargas Street she had inherited from her father. While this move in 1923 solved some immediate financial problems, Fremont was still in a state of deep depression. His gloom and despair so permeated the house that the only place where Lencha could find solace was at the cathedral where she went often and prayed to St. Anthony to help her husband out of his agony.

Fremont now had to face the fact that he might not ever support himself or his family solely through his painting. This was a hard realization to accept. He knew he had to do something, so he thought he would start by giving himself one more chance with one last painting. This painting would be just the way he wanted it, regardless of what anyone else might think or say about it. Lencha was pleased with the decision, and she encouraged Fremont to follow his heart's work. His wife was always his inspiration and the rock on which he leaned as they faced their early challenges and discouragements.

For three or four weeks he worked day and night on the painting which depicted a winter scene of hills and pine trees lit with the last rays of the sun. An *arroyo* was shadowed in the foreground. He titled it, *When Evening Comes*. Because he was working in such cramped quarters, he was not able to properly view his entire 40 x 50 inches canvas until the painting was finished and taken to the Fine Arts Museum and hung on the wall.

After evaluating this "final creation," he decided it was acceptable and went home, planning to return the next day to quietly give the painting another critique. When he arrived at the museum the following day, he was dumbfounded by the surprising news that this last work of art—his supposed swan song as a landscape painter—had created quite a stir. Better yet, a buyer was willing to pay an unheard of purchase price of six hundred dollars for it. Moreover, it was stipulated that the artist could exhibit the painting where he chose until the buyer could arrange an appropriate space for it, and should it win any awards in the meantime, the artist could keep the prize money.

The painting was bought by Frank Springer, a man who worked with the group who raised the money to finance the building of the Fine Arts Museum in Santa Fe. Springer was a lawyer who came from Iowa to New Mexico in 1873 and stayed to help develop this territory of immense beauty and natural resources. He became the president of the Maxwell Land Grant Company which included over 1.7 million acres, and he lived in Cimarron and Springer, New Mexico, before settling in Las Vegas, an old Spanish town about sixty miles north of Santa Fe. He was active in civic and state affairs. He helped lay the foundations of New Mexico Highlands University in Las Vegas, New Mexico, the Art Museum of New Mexico in Santa Fe, and other cultural institutions in the state. He was very interested in supporting local artists, and he gave the Ellis painting to his nephew who lived on the Springer Ranch in Cimarron, New Mexico. Later it was donated to the Museum of Fine Arts in Santa Fe, New Mexico. Fremont Ellis knew personally that "Frank Springer was a man of great accomplishment" as he was so described by William I. Ausich, Ohio State University.

When Evening Comes was the turning point in Fremont's art career. He later stated, "From then on I was always able to sell enough to live fairly well. I can't complain. Very well, in fact."

Meanwhile, through his contacts in Los Angeles, Fremont entered the painting in the 1924 Spring Exhibition at the Los Angeles Museum where he was awarded the Henry E. Huntington Prize for best landscape in the show.

The prize put Fremont Ellis on the map and made others take notice. With this new beginning, Fremont and his family were able to return to their home on the Camino, and he continued to paint and exhibit his works in local, regional, and national shows. Life was good and getting better.

The birth of a son, Frederick Ellis, in 1924 added to his joy. He was inspired to greater heights in his painting, and more exciting opportunities began to come his way.

Later that year in November Fremont entered another painting, *A Gathering Storm,* in an exhibition at the Los Angeles Museum. This evaluation of his painting by columnist Anthony Anderson appeared in a 1924 newspaper in Los Angeles under his column, "Of Art and Artists."

> Come we now to Herculean vigor in paint, a masculine attack that knocks the spots out of everything around it. We find it in Fremont Ellis and A. H. Knott, and, to a lesser degree, in a few others. No pretty sentiment about these painters, believe me. They wrestle long and hard with big brushes charged thick with paint and emerge from the fray calm and triumphant. *Gathering Storm* by Fremont Ellis is one of the outstanding

pictures in the Exhibition. Somber, almost forbidding in its dark intensity, it is yet big in effect, a transcript from Nature that holds the brooding temperament of the artist. Ellis paints like no other man that we know of. His forceful originality compels your attention and admiration.

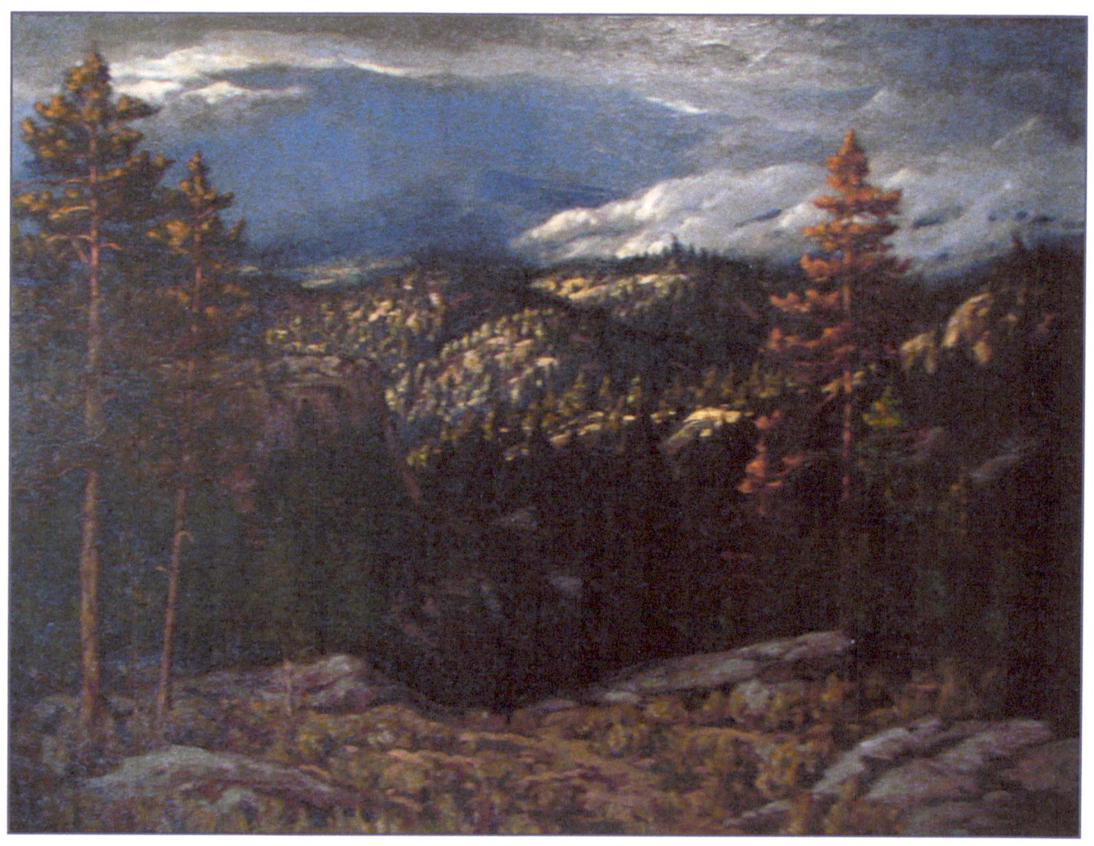

A Gathering Storm is owned by the St. Francis Hotel in Santa Fe, New Mexico and hangs in its lobby. Oil Painting, 50 x 60 inches. Courtesy of St Francis Hotel in Santa Fe, New Mexico.

Los Cinco Pintores existed during the Prohibition Era. To have the drinks they needed for their parties, some of the group made their own beer and whiskey. Stories have been told of their constant fear of the revenue officer and how they sometimes had to pull the plug in a bathtub full of their brew before the suspicious officer got there to inspect their homes. At other times they moved their pots of illegal brew from one house to another during his visits.

Fremont Ellis did not drink as much as his friends, and he never made any liquor. He was basically a very serious man who found the life-style of his friends amusing and relaxing after a long day of creative concentration, but he was too shy and reserved to join wholeheartedly in their wild antics.

Will Shuster, who was Ellis' best friend, was the entertainer of the group. He was a natural comedian who loved to perform. His skits and pantomimes were of professional caliber. Fremont especially loved watching him. Shuster was also the creator of Zozobra, or Old Man Gloom, in 1924. His creation still goes up in flames in the Santa Fe skies at Fiesta time each year. For *Los Cinco Pintores,* all the troubles and worries of the proceeding year disappeared in smoke and flames with the destruction of Old Man Gloom.

Will Shuster first conceived and created Zozobra as the focus of a private fiesta at his home for artists and writers in the community. Shuster and E. Dana Johnson, a newspaper editor, came up with the name Zozobra, which was defined as "anguish, anxiety, and misery." Shuster assigned all rights, title, and interest in Zozobra on June 19, 1964, to the Kiwanis Club of Santa Fe. Every year since that time the Kiwanis Club stages the burning of Will Shuster's Zozobra to symbolically erase all hardships and travails of the past year. Since 1952, the show has raised over $300,000 which the Kiwanis Foundation has used to provide college scholarships and local youth projects and camp fees for physically handicapped children.

When Shuster died in 1969, Ellis painted a picture of his funeral. The sadness and bleakness of the picture strikingly reflect the deep pain and loss Ellis felt upon the passing of this great friend. The painting now hangs in the Museum of Fine Arts in Santa Fe, New Mexico.

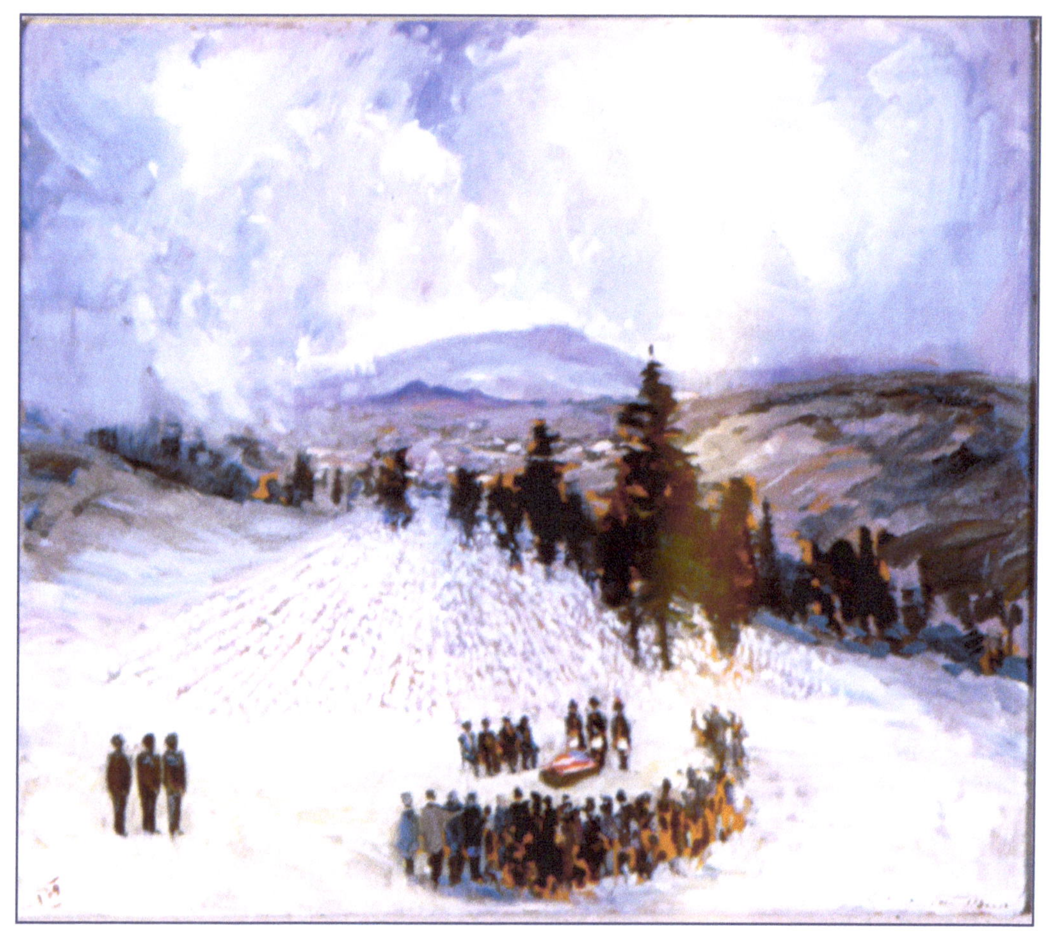

Adios Amigo—Hasta La Vista, 1969, oil on canvas painting of the funeral of Will Shuster. 25 x 30 inches. Collection of the Museum of Fine Art, Santa Fe, New Mexico. Gift of Fremont F. Ellis, 1969.

Los Cinco Pintores quietly disbanded in 1926 when Nash and Mruk left the area. It was a friendly parting, and all remained close friends. It had been a very rewarding experience, especially for Fremont Ellis who continued to live and work in Santa Fe.

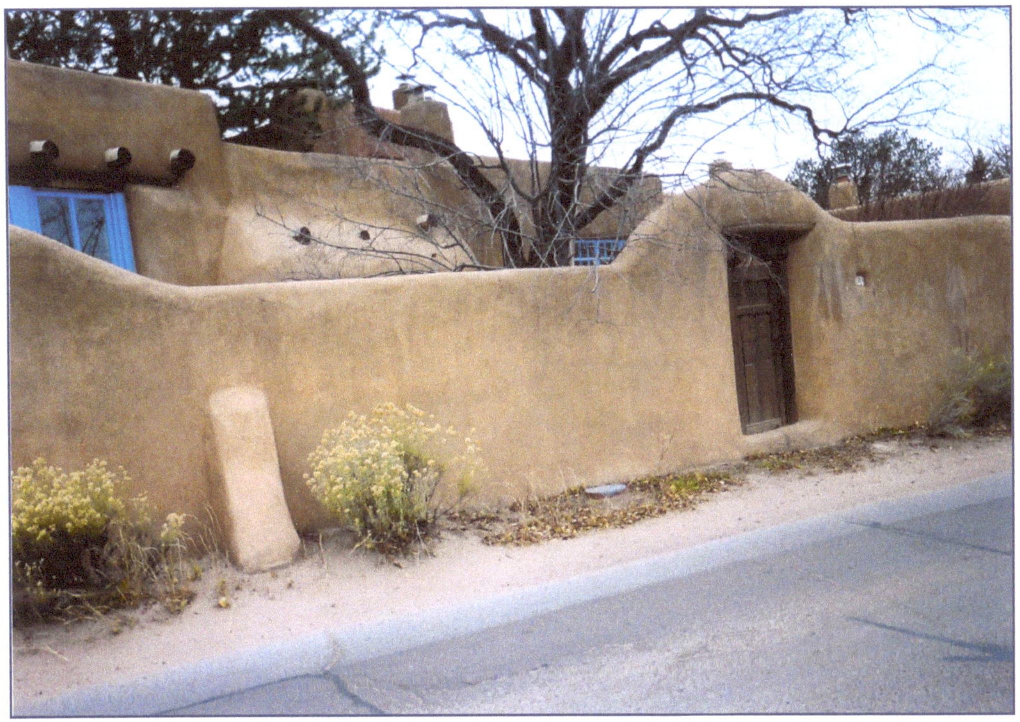

Front view of the house that Fremont Ellis built for his family on Camino del Monte Sol in Santa Fe, New Mexico. It was originally one room, but additions in later years made the structure into a large beautiful Southwestern home. Photograph by Barbara Foster.

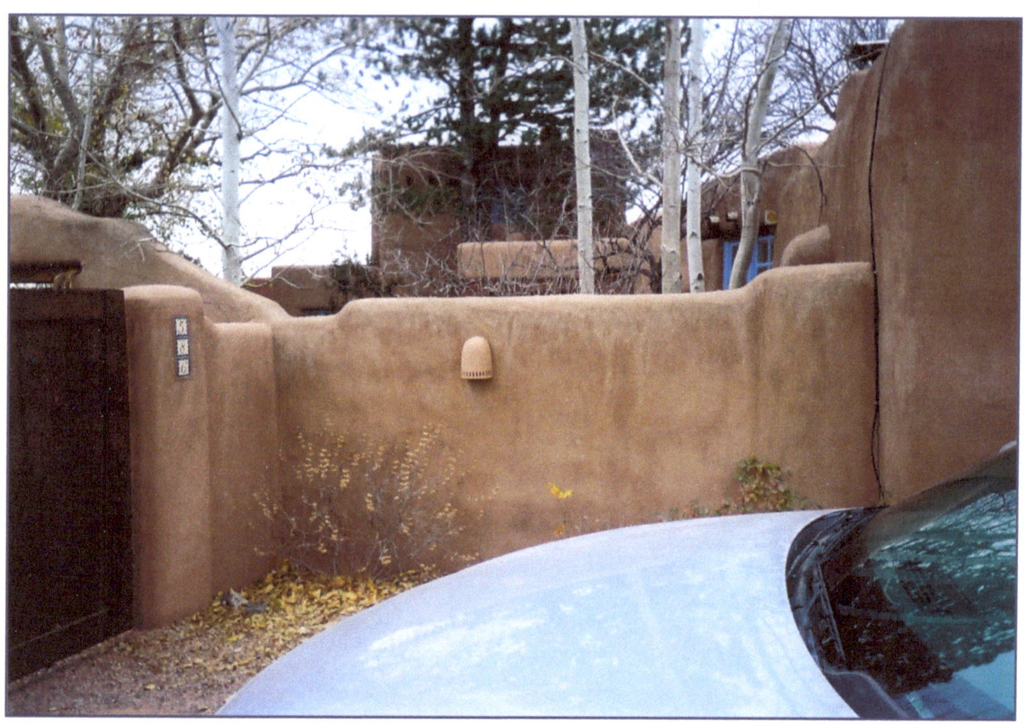

Back view of house that Fremont Ellis built on Camino del Monte Sol in Santa Fe.
Studio is taller structure in background.
Photograph by Barbara Foster.

The decade of the 1930s was a time of growth, professionally and financially for the Ellis family. In 1939 Oscar Love who was President of the Albuquerque National Bank and a great admirer of Ellis' paintings, struck a deal with Fremont. The bank owned the six hundred acre San Sebastian Land Grant which was located between Santa Fe and Pecos on the Lamy cutoff, and since Ellis felt he needed more space, the banker offered to trade him the land for six of his paintings. Fremont now became a land owner, and looked forward to a new and inspirational life style where he and Lencha could raise their family and build a magnificent hacienda and studio.

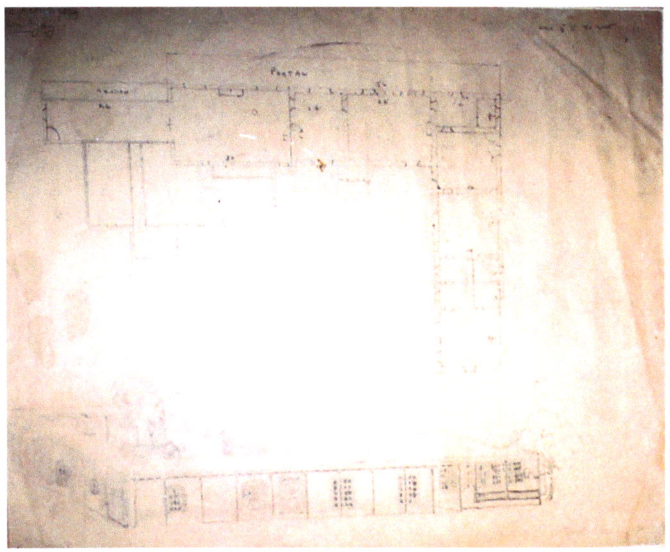

The hand-drawn plans of the hacienda Fremont Ellis planned to build on his land. Photograph courtesy of Bambi Ellis.

Fremont started work on his ranch home project in 1939. The house on Camino del Monte Sol was rented and the family moved into a tent set up on the mountain acres, and Fremont started his building program. He used materials from the abandoned ruins of a log cabin to build his own log cabin where he lived while he built the remainder of the house. The cabin was originally a stage coach stop on the Santa Fe Trail. Lencha and the children reclaimed their house in Santa Fe in the winter so the children could go to school.

Bambi graduated from the Loretto Academy in May of 1940. Fremont and Lencha planned a graduation party for their daughter in the patio of their spacious new *hacienda.* Along with an assortment of food for the guests, they also listened and danced to the music of La Fonda Orchestra from Santa Fe under the direction of Billy Palou. The famous guitarist, Gonzalo Lujan from Mexico, also played that night, as well as the charismatic pianist, Fred Baldez. It was a gala graduation night for Bambi Ellis as well as an impressive housewarming for the new ranch home of the Ellis family, *La Hacienda de San Sebastian.*

EARLY PAINTINGS of FREMONT F. ELLIS

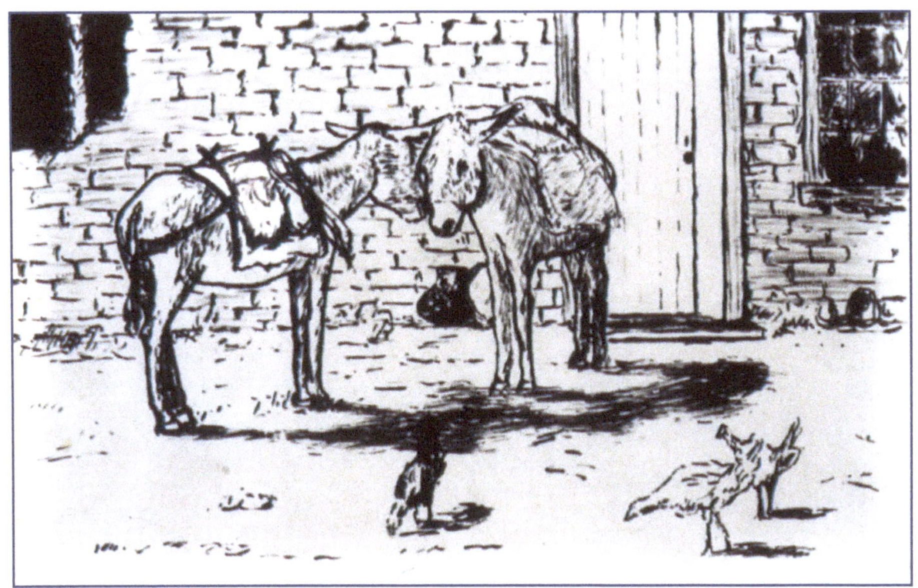

Los Compadres, photo-etching on white wove paper in early 1920s, 4 x 6 1/4 inches. Collection of the Museum of Fine Art, Santa Fe, New Mexico. Gift of Gerald P. Peters, 1974.

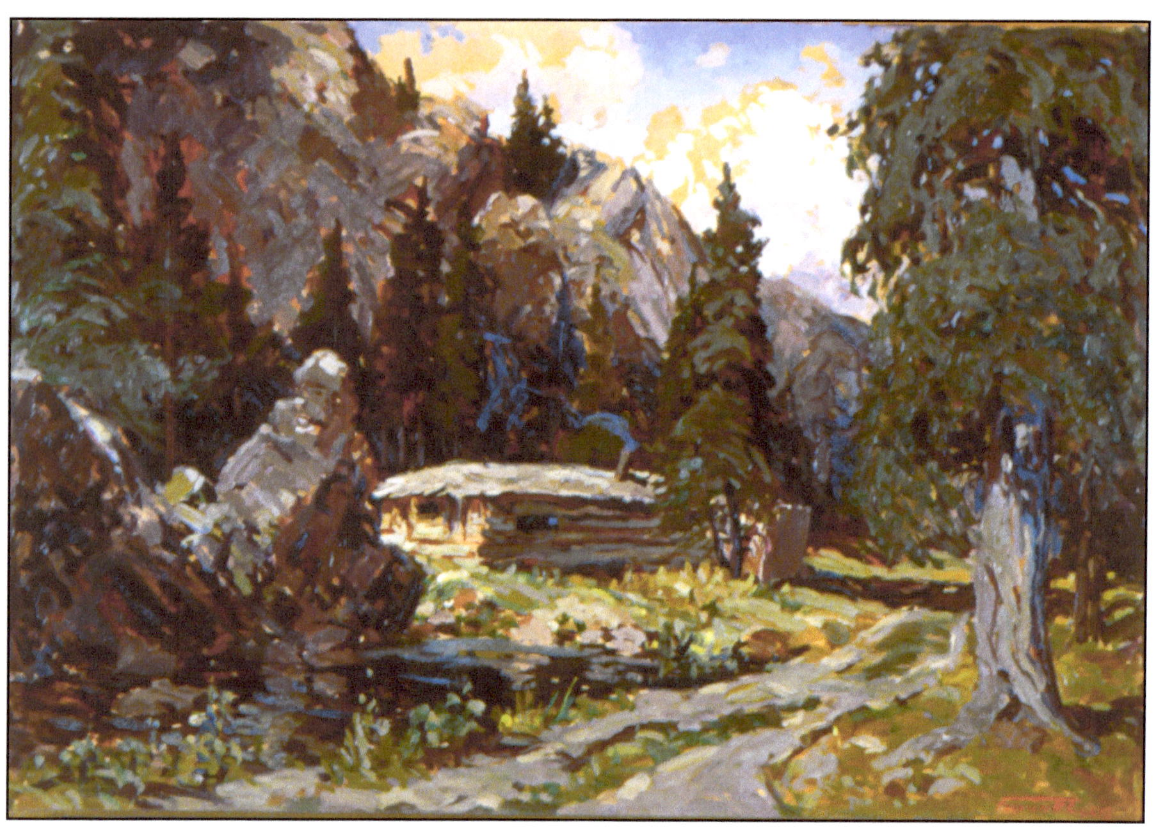

Old Trapper's Cabin, Red River Canyon, circa 1927, oil on paperboard, 26 x 39 inches.
Collection of the New Mexico Museum of Fine Art, Santa Fe, New Mexico.
Gift of Mrs. Irene Fabri in memory of Edith W. Proebstel, 1965.

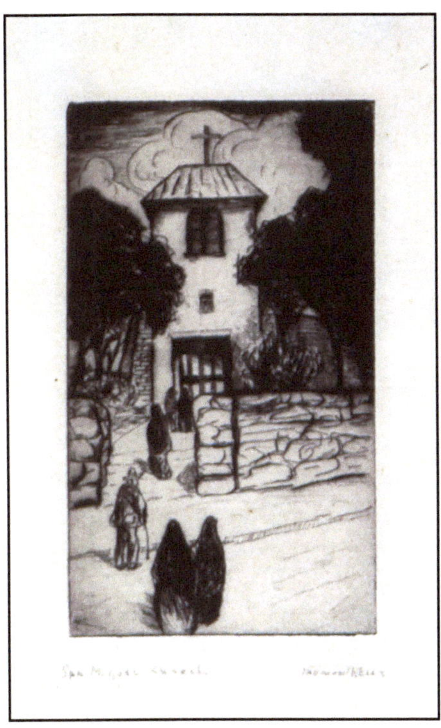

San Miguel Church, Santa Fe, n.d., etching, 5 1/4 by 3 1/4 inches. Collection of the New Mexico Museum of Fine Art, Santa Fe, New Mexico. Gift of Mrs. E. G. Trowbridge, 193l.

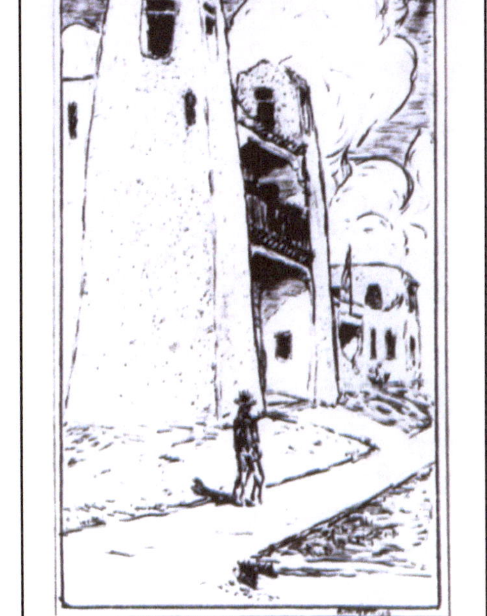

The New Museum, Santa Fe, circa 1917, etching, 5 1/4 x 3 1/8 inches. Collection of the New Mexico Museum of Fine Art, Santa Fe, New Mexico. Gift of Fremont F. Ellis, 1964.

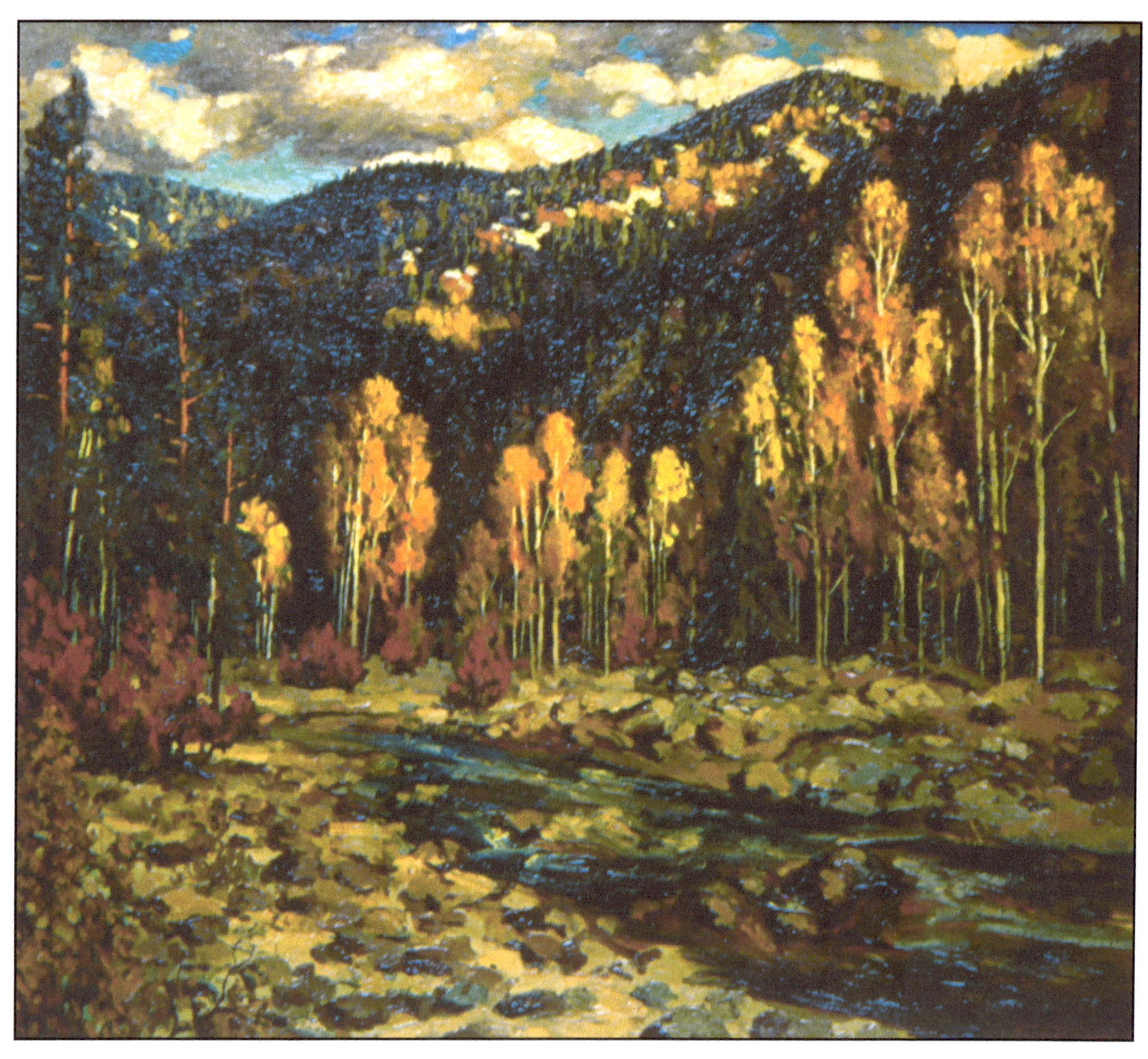

The Trout Stream, 1925, oil on canvas, 26 x 30 inches.
Collection of the Stark Museum of Art, Orange, Texas. 31 20/28.

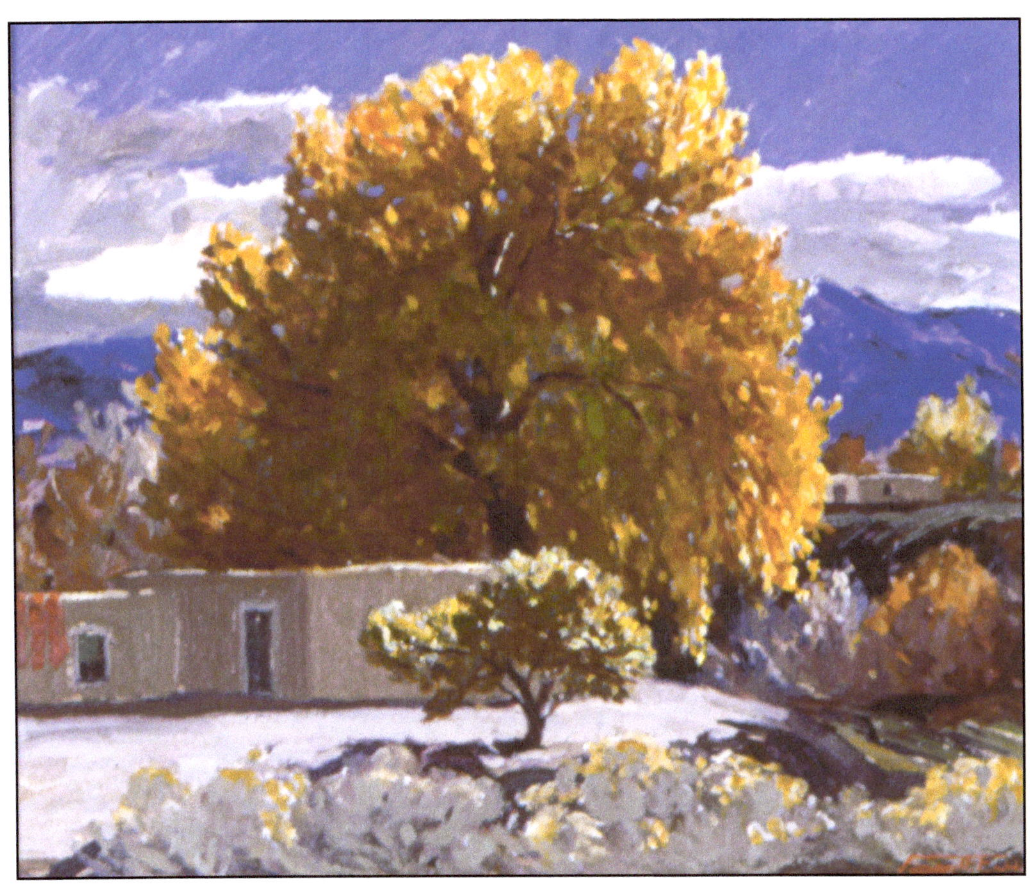

Adobe with Trees, n.d., oil on canvas, 16 x 20 inches.
Collection of the Museum of Fine Art, Santa Fe, New Mexico.
Gift of Mildred N. Heady Estate, 2001.

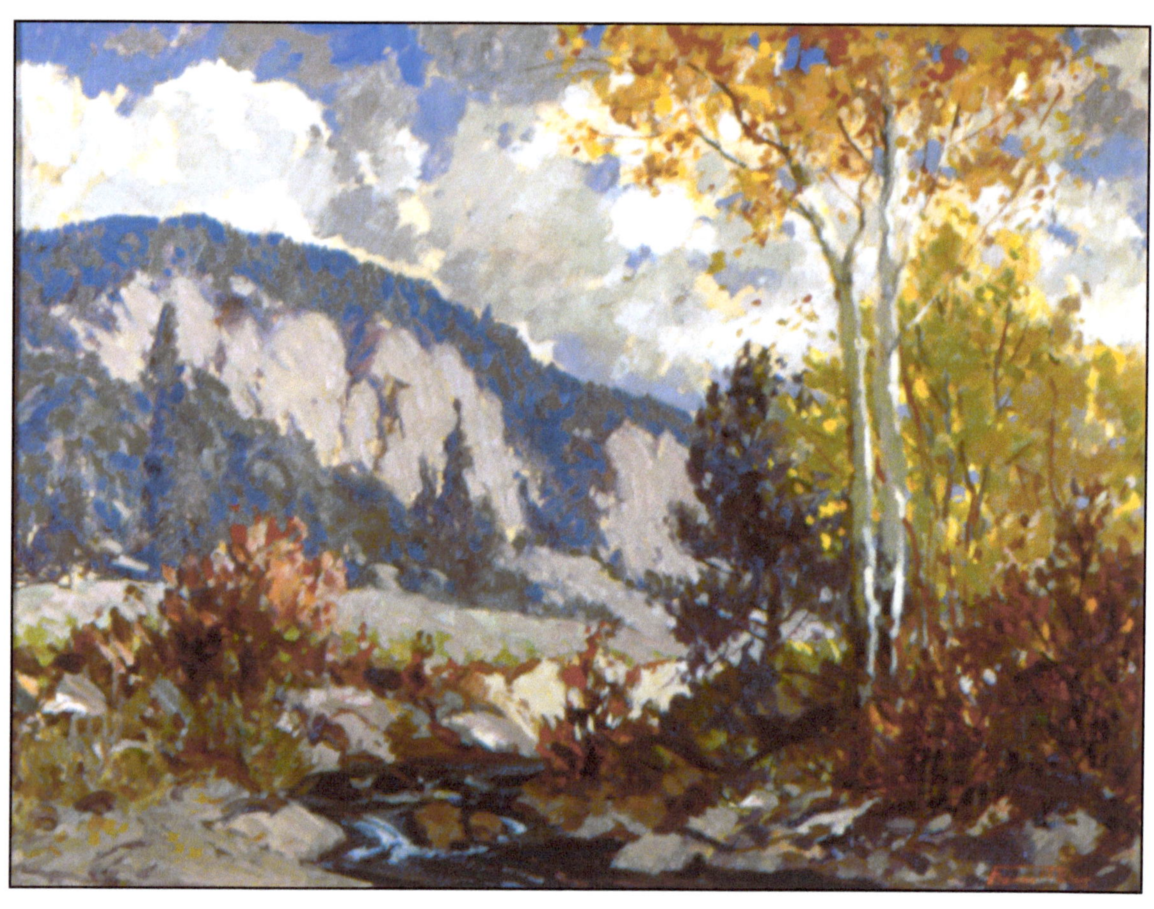

Mountain Landscape, n.d., oil on canvas, 19 x 27 inches.
Collection of the Museum of Fine Art, Santa Fe, New Mexico.
Gift of Mildred N. Heady Estate, 2001.

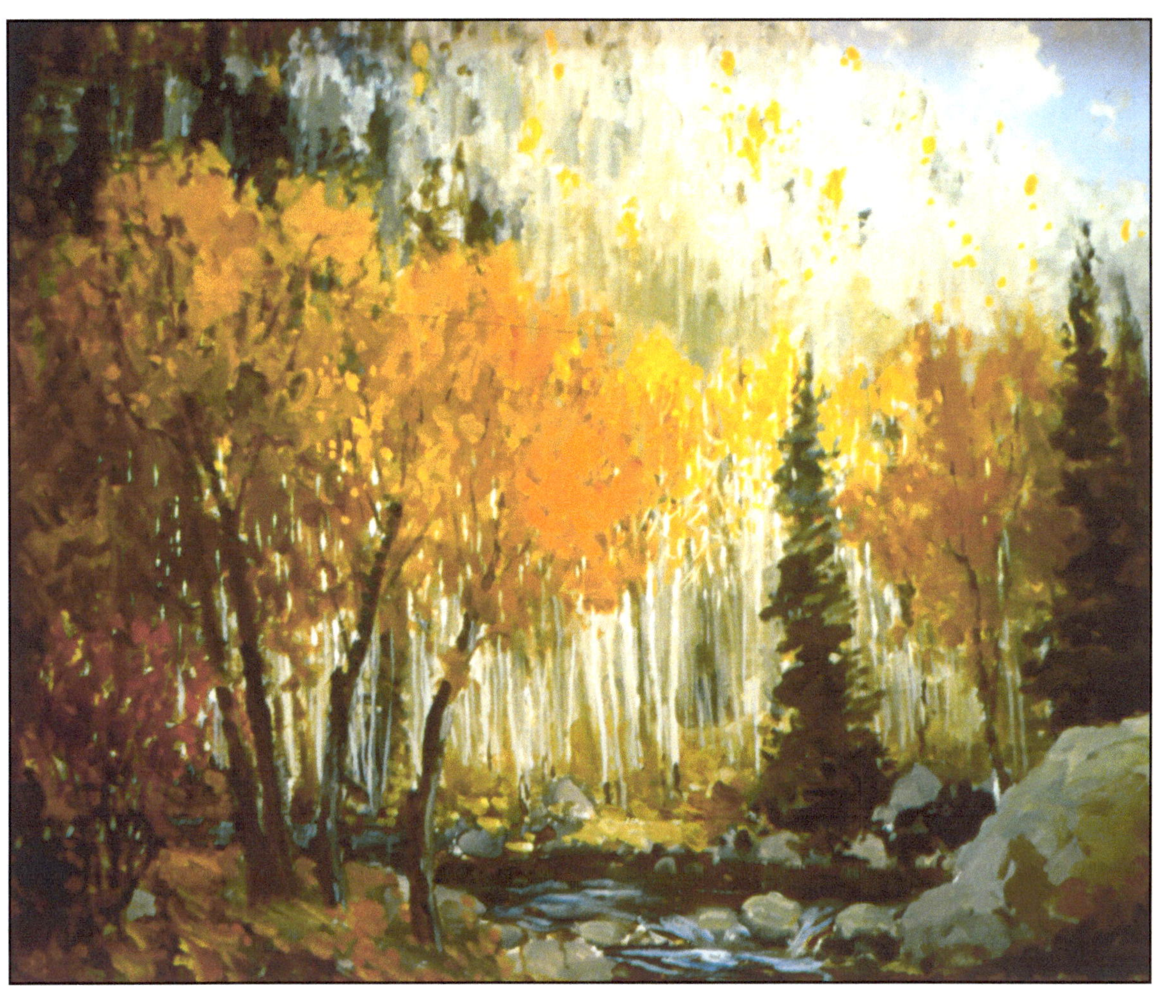

Near Tres Ritos, n.d., liquitex on canvas, 25 1/8 x 29 7/8 inches. Accession no. 1977.25.1.
Collection of the El Paso Museum of Art, El Paso, Texas. Gift of W. R. Weaver Co.

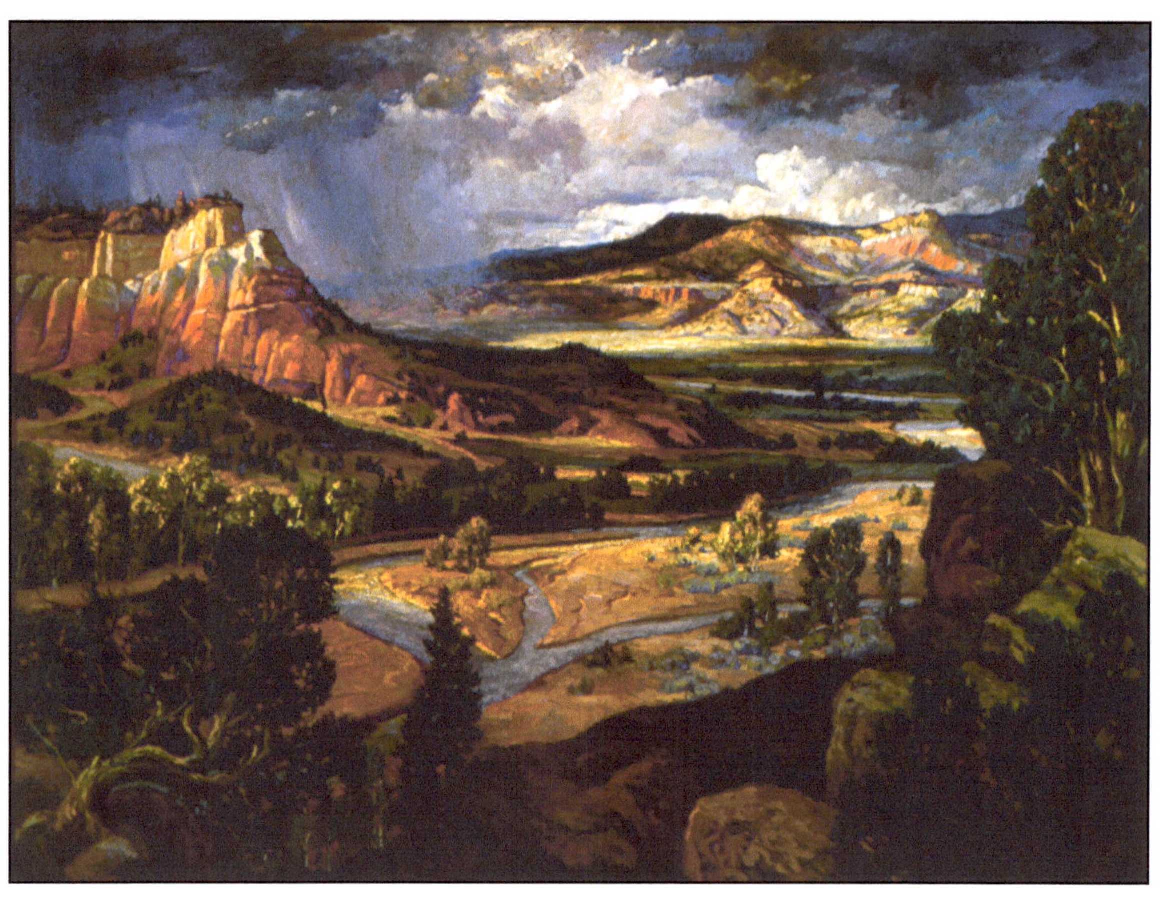

Valley of the Gods, 1926, oil on canvas, 59 x 78 inches. Accession no. 1959.160.1.
Collection of the El Paso Museum of Art, El Paso, Texas.

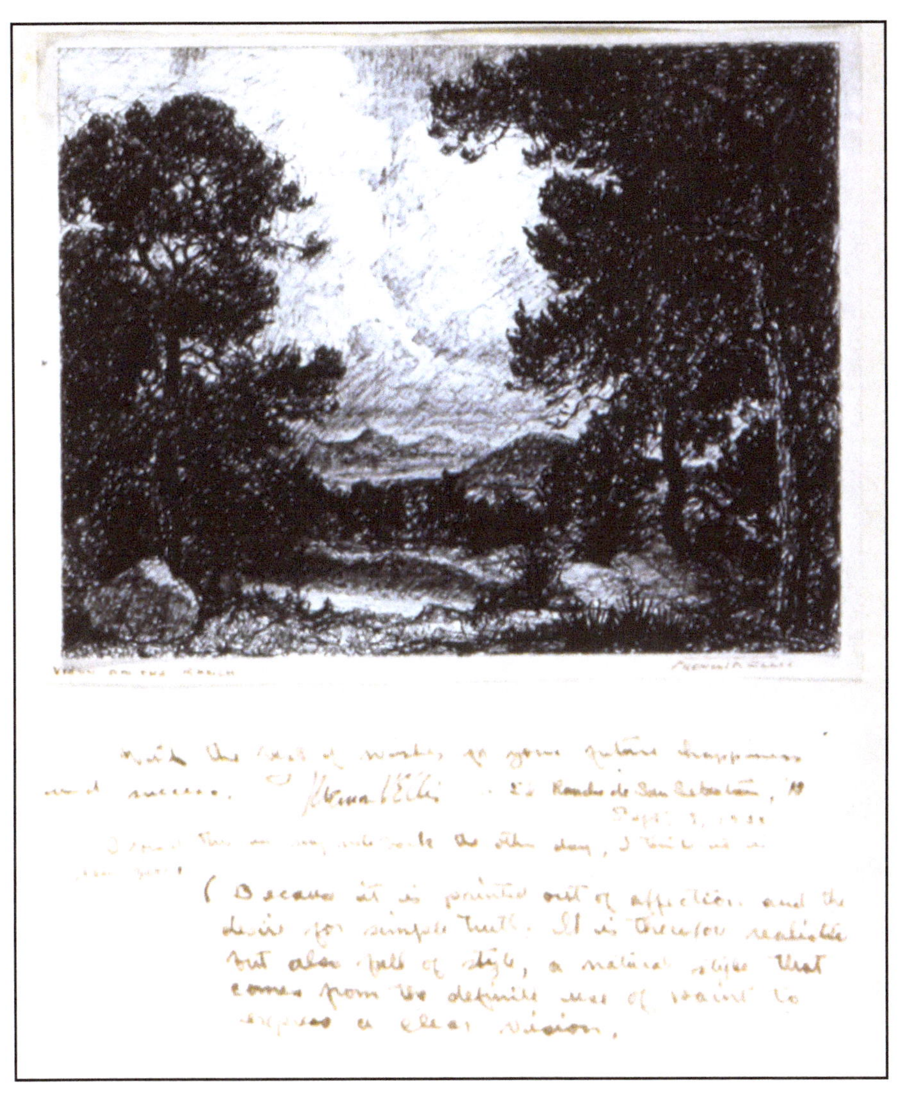

View of the Ranch, 1933, ink on paper, 12 x 9 inches.
Collection of the Museum of Fine Art, Santa Fe, New Mexico. Museum purchase, 1986.

10

LA HACIENDA *de* SAN SEBASTIAN

Back when Harper Henry had begun construction on his home, Fremont had been fascinated with his ability as an architect and builder. Fremont thought Henry would be the perfect person to assist him with his own ideas for the unusual home he wanted. His plan for his new home was to dismantle and transport two old existing structures to the site. The mud adobes of an old adobe *hacienda* some sixteen miles away in Galisteo would become part of his home, and for his studio, he wanted to retrieve and use the adobes from the abandoned ruins of a church in Galisteo.

The *hacienda* in Galisteo had belonged to Don Pedro Bautista Pino, a distinguished *alcalde* (mayor) and resident of the Santa Fe area noted for his integrity, compassion, devotion to civic and military duties, and his wealth. He was a prominent rancher, a military commandant, and a civic and political leader who was the representative of the King of Spain. He had spared no expense when he built the *hacienda* in Galisteo for a retreat from his many duties.

The *hacienda* had been built over one hundred years ago and had been uninhabited for many years, but the sturdy adobes, which were large and thick, were still in almost perfect shape. As the adobes, vigas, windows with mica panes, wooden shutters—all of the old building—were moved to the new building site, Fremont made an architectural drawing so the *hacienda* would be rebuilt as an exact replica of what it had been in its early days.

Harper Henry supervised the adobe-by-adobe move of the old *hacienda* as well as the adobes of the old church in Galisteo. He then planned and coordinated their meticulous reconstruction, integrating the two structures into what became *La Hacienda de San Sebastian*, one of the most beautiful country homes in the Santa Fe area.

Had Fremont Ellis not been a painter, he would probably have become a successful architect or construction contractor. He had felt a real sense of fulfillment when he built his first adobe home on Camino del Monte Sol and now, with his added maturity and experience and the help of his friend, Harper Henry, he was able to create his version of a Southwestern home with porticos and vigas, and fireplaces. By trading paintings, he collected antique Spanish furniture as well as antique Louis XV French furniture from a dealer in El Paso who had gotten the pieces in New Orleans. He continued to add to his antique furniture through the years as he had many rooms to fill.

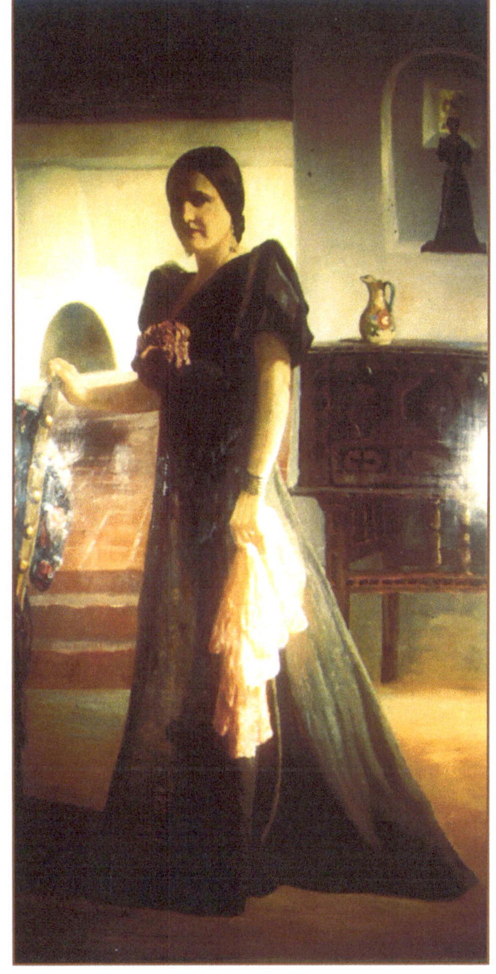

A 1940 painting of Laurencita Gonzales de Ellis standing in the living room of her new ranch home. Note the influence of the seventeenth century Spanish painter, Velazquez, whom Ellis admired. The floor of the entranceway was constructed of handmade bricks. Photograph courtesy of Frederick Ellis.

When the family moved into their new home in 1940, the historical old adobes from Don Pedro's *hacienda* and the old church provided a lavish home, and it echoed to the young voices of Bambi and Freddie and their friends. Fremont painted with new life and vigor, and he also continued working on their new home, adding improvements as new ideas came to his mind. Corrals were built, horses were bought, and fields were plowed and planted. *La Hacienda de San Sebastian* evolved into a truly great ranch, home, and studio.

Meanwhile, Harper Henry had purchased land from Ellis across the way. Other artists followed, including Helmuth Naumer, Tom Lea, and Pansy Stockton—all settling on what became San Sebastian Ranch, a place of friendship and fellowship. Later Lord and Lady Rupert Samuelson from England also joined the artistic group.

Pansy Stockton was an artist who used fragments of hundreds of varieties of vegetations as mediums in her work. Some of her pictures had as many as 10,000 components, and she worked with many kinds of vegetation from all over the world. She called her creations sun paintings. Pansy was a personable woman with a wonderful sense of humor. She became quite famous and was interviewed by Ralph Edwards, well known radio personality at that time.

Tom Lea, a fine artist, did a painting of Ellis' daughter, Bambi, in exchange for land to build a house. Bee Binkley built a house on Ellis land with the help of Harper Henry. Her daughter, Betty, took art lessons from Fremont Ellis for many years. She became a well-known Santa Fe artist. Helmuth Naumer sold many of his pastels to the actress, Greer Garson, who had a home near Pecos, New Mexico. So, the ranch became quite an artists' community, along with one writer, Earl Scott, who wrote mystery novels.

San Sebastian became the hub for all the creative friends of Fremont and Lencha and their children. Henry even built them a swimming pool which was a gathering place for all the neighbors.

All through the 1940s, Fremont followed his painting routine, but he also suffered periods of frustration in which he periodically gave up painting. He always regrouped, however, and gave himself time to improve his work.

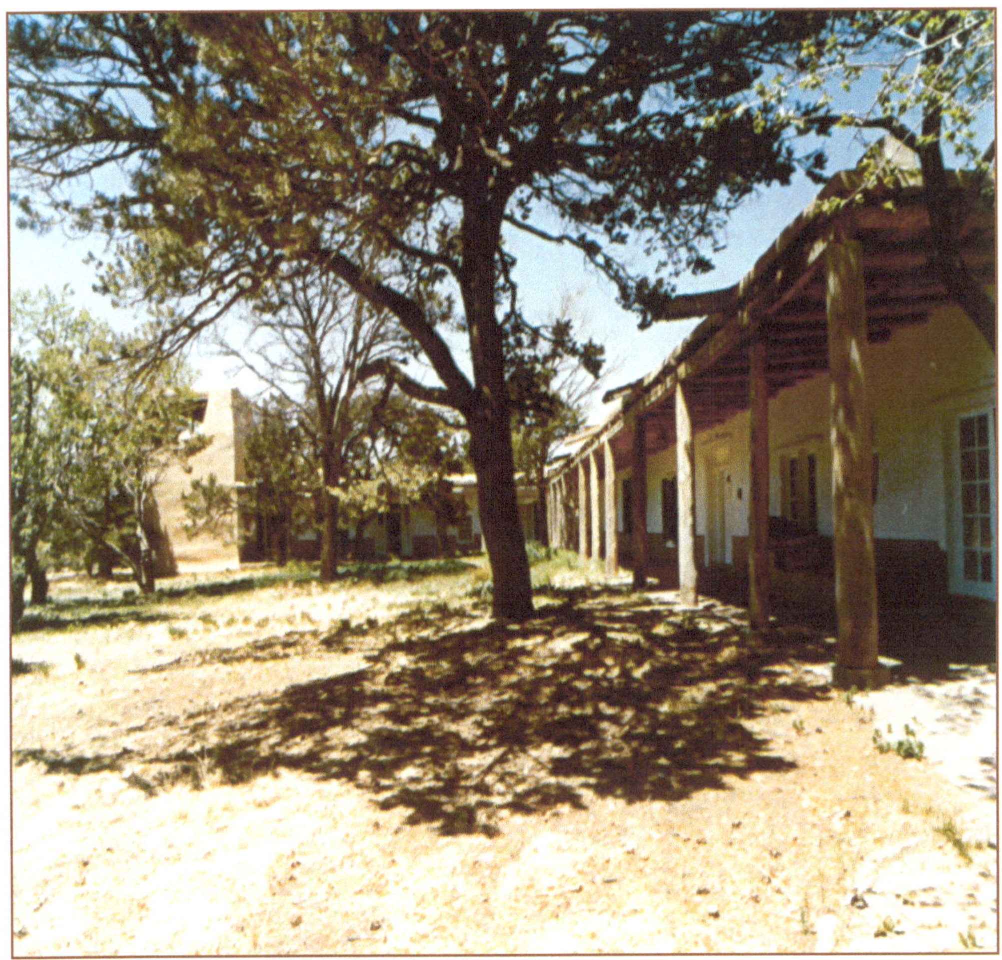

The completed ranch home of the Ellis family. Photograph courtesy of Bambi Ellis.

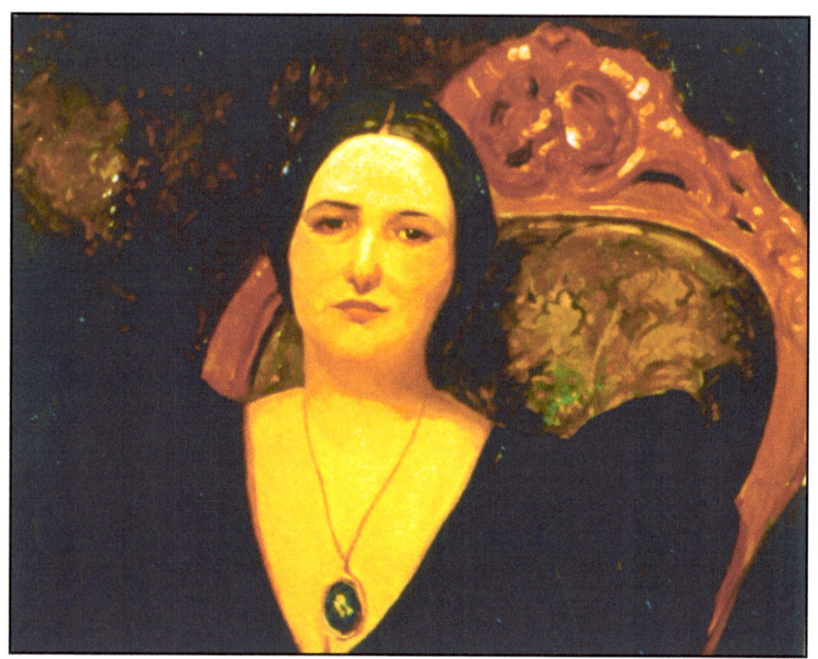

Another painting of Laurencita Gonzales de Ellis. Photograph courtesy of Bambi Ellis.

In the late 1940s, the United States Steamship Line contacted Fremont Ellis and commissioned him to paint a large New Mexico landscape for their new luxury liner, the S.S. America. The interior was a uniquely American atmosphere. The painting would hang in the library on the first class deck of the spacious ship.

Ellis chose the Abiquiu, New Mexico, area as the setting for his painting. The finished product was a spectacular canyon landscape of rocks, hills, bluffs, and the breathtaking terrain of unique and colorful New Mexico.

The S.S. America made only its maiden voyage and one more trip before

World War II began, and it was then converted into a Navy transport ship which carried over 300,000 servicemen and women safely back and forth from the war zones. In 1946 the S.S. America was restored to her pre-war brilliance and sailed triumphantly into New York to start transatlantic service. It was considered the most beautiful of all American passenger ships.

Fremont Ellis later heard from several servicemen and passengers who had traveled on the S.S. America and had enjoyed the New Mexico painting, thanking him for his wonderful painting which inspired their interest in New Mexico.

At this same time, the Atchison, Topeka, and the Santa Fe Railroad commissioned Fremont to do a painting which would hang in their administrative office in Chicago. A copy of the painting was also put on the menus in the dining cars on their passenger trains. The painting was a study of golden yellow aspen trees in the fall.

Fremont Ellis's reputation as a well known and outstanding southwestern painter was becoming recognized worldwide.

PAINTINGS CREATED DURING FREMONT F. ELLIS' PRODUCTIVE YEARS

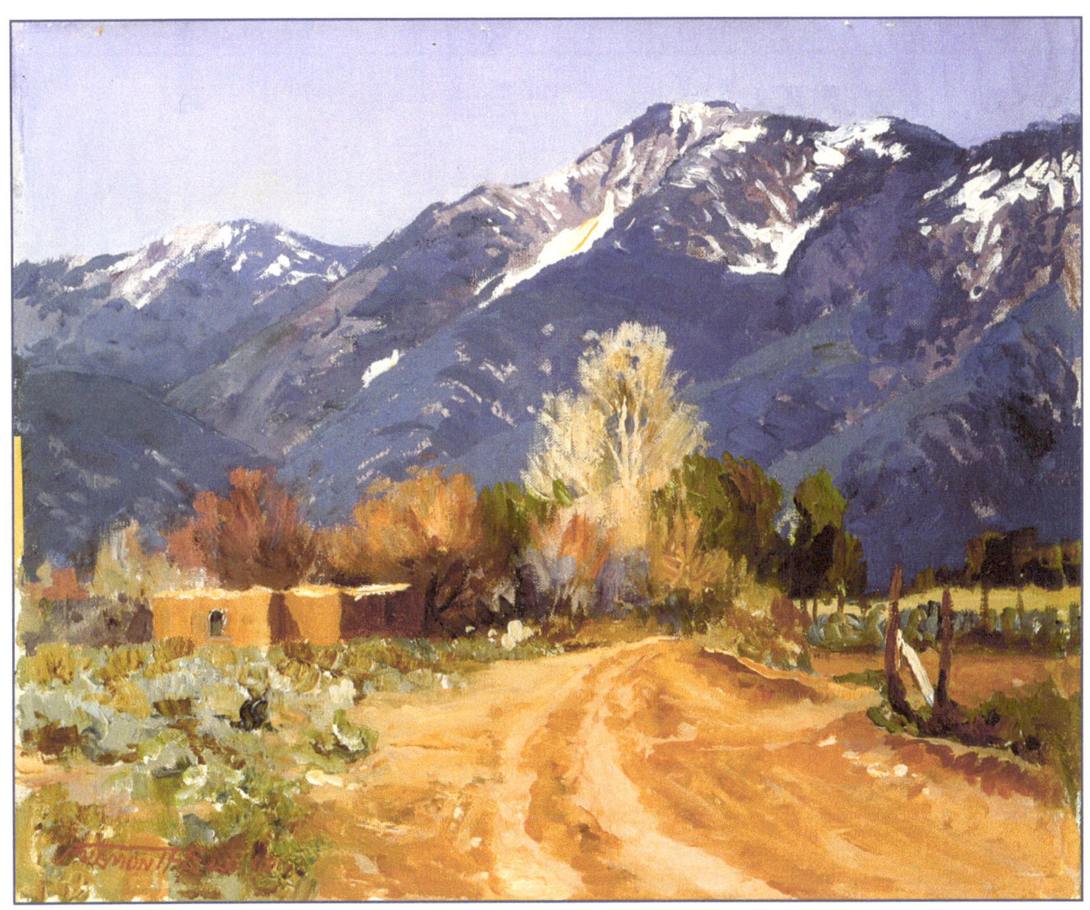

Early Spring, Arroyo Hondo, Taos, New Mexico, c. 1953, oil on canvas, 25 x 30 inches.
Collection of the Stark Museum of Art, Orange, Texas. 31.20/2

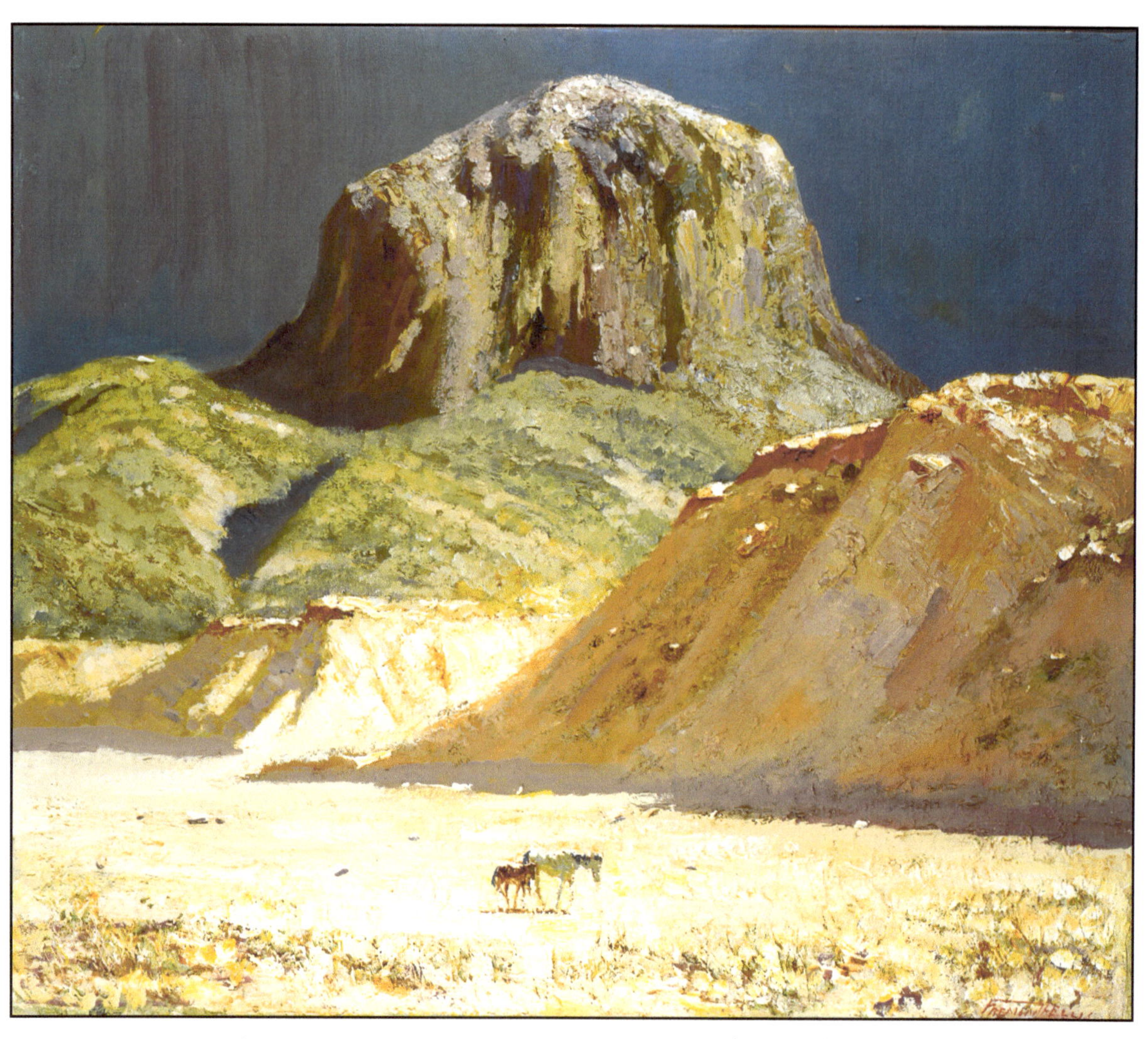

Storm over Cabezon Peak, oil on canvasboard, 24 7/8 x 29 7/8 inches.
Collection of the Stark Museum of Art, Orange, Texas. 31.20/3

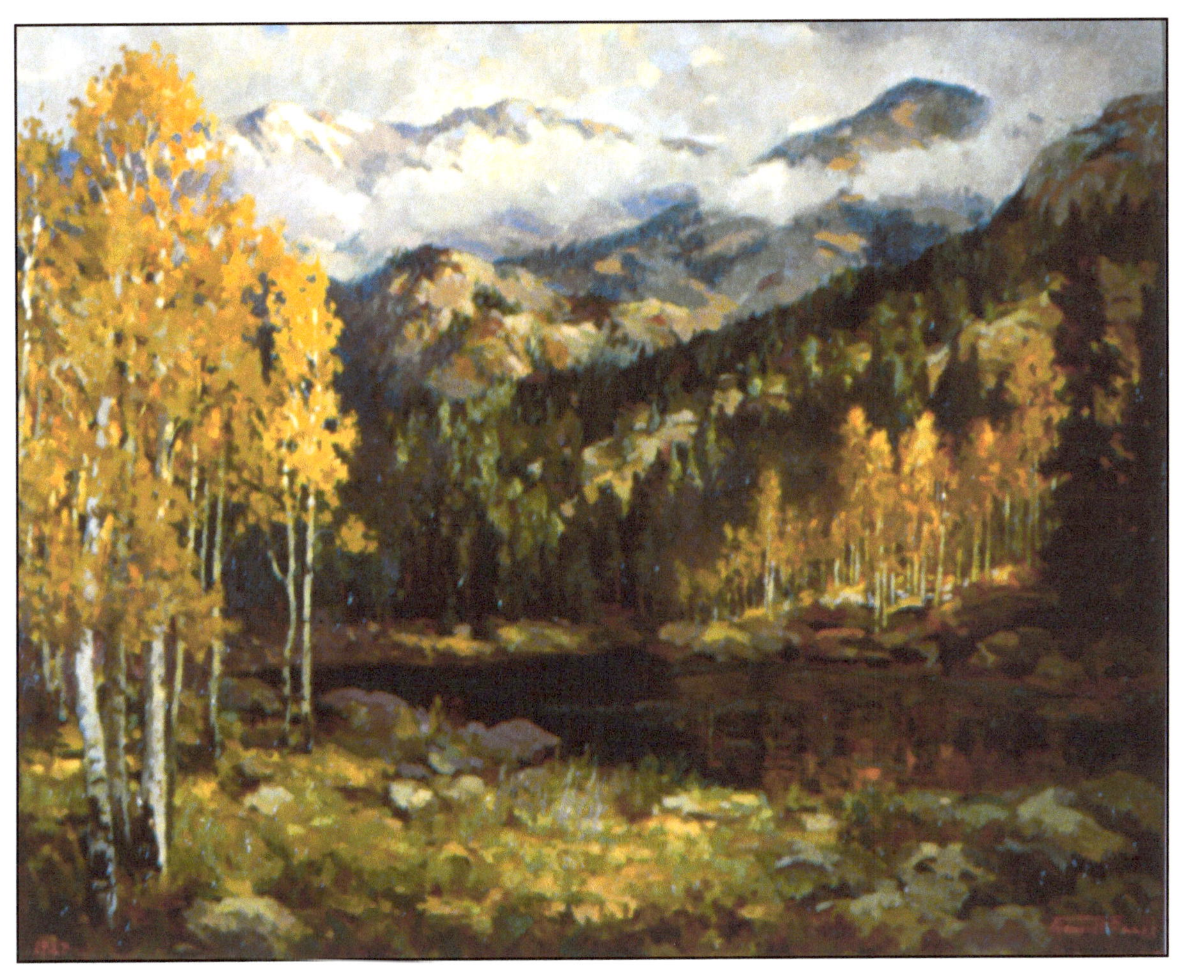

Mist after a Storm, 1927, oil on canvas, 27 x 34 1/2 inches.
Collection of the Museum of Fine Art, Santa Fe, New Mexico.
Gift of Mrs. John A. Hurley, 1966.

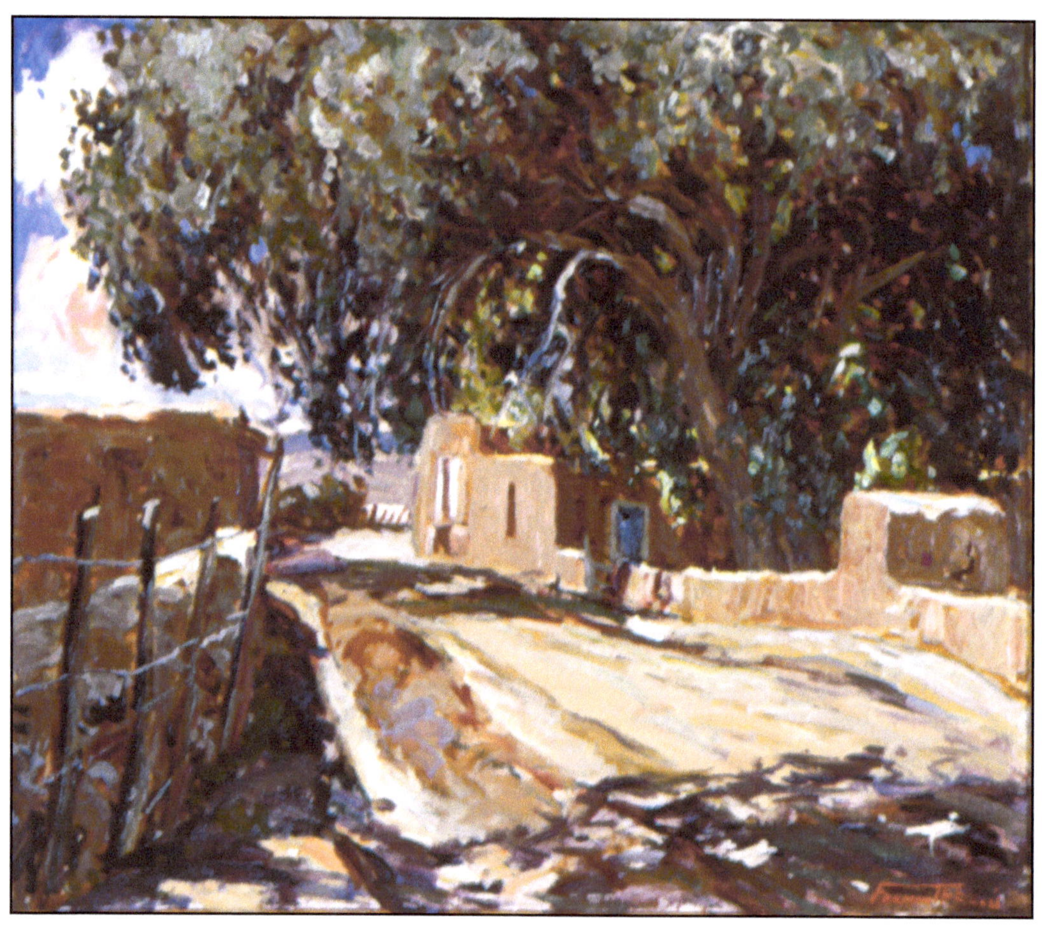

Street Scene, Galisteo, circa 1934, oil on canvas board, 20 x 24 inches.
On long term loan to the Museum of Art, Santa Fe, New Mexico, from the
U.S. General Services Administration, Federal Emergency Relief Administration.

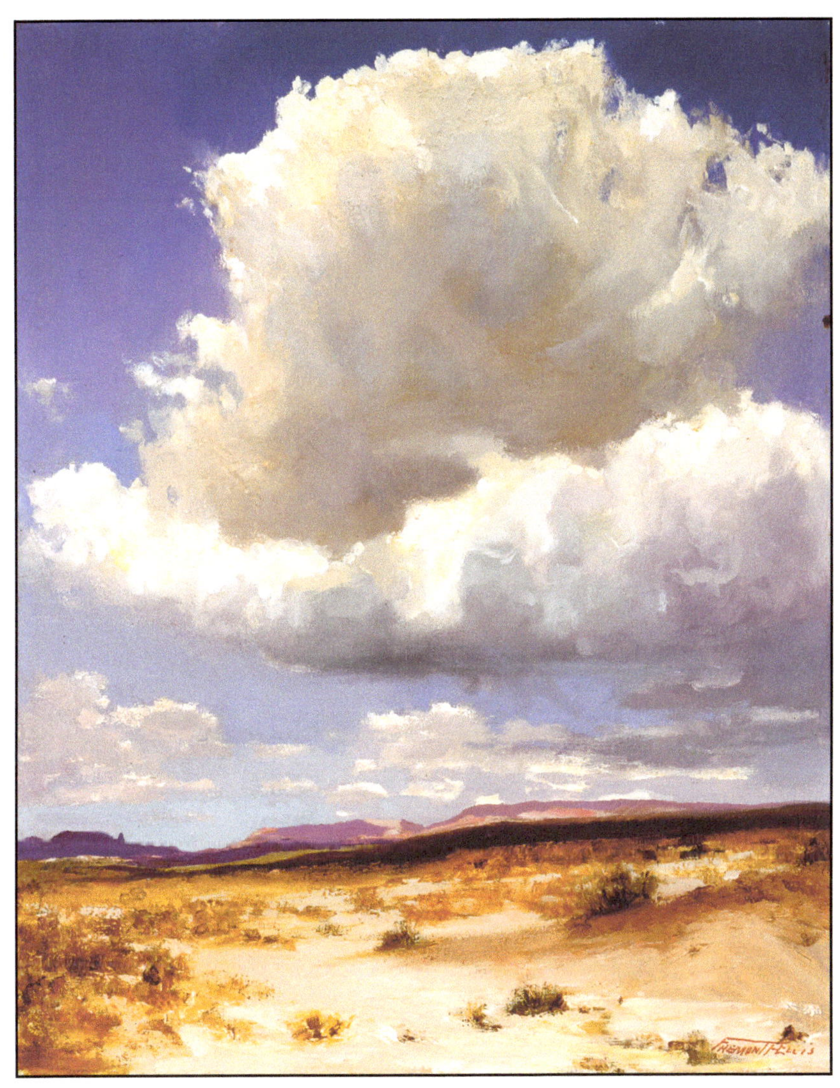

Summer Clouds, New Mexico, c. 1953, oil on canvas. 25 x 20 1/8 inches.
Collection of the Stark Museum of Art, Orange Texas. 31.20/16.

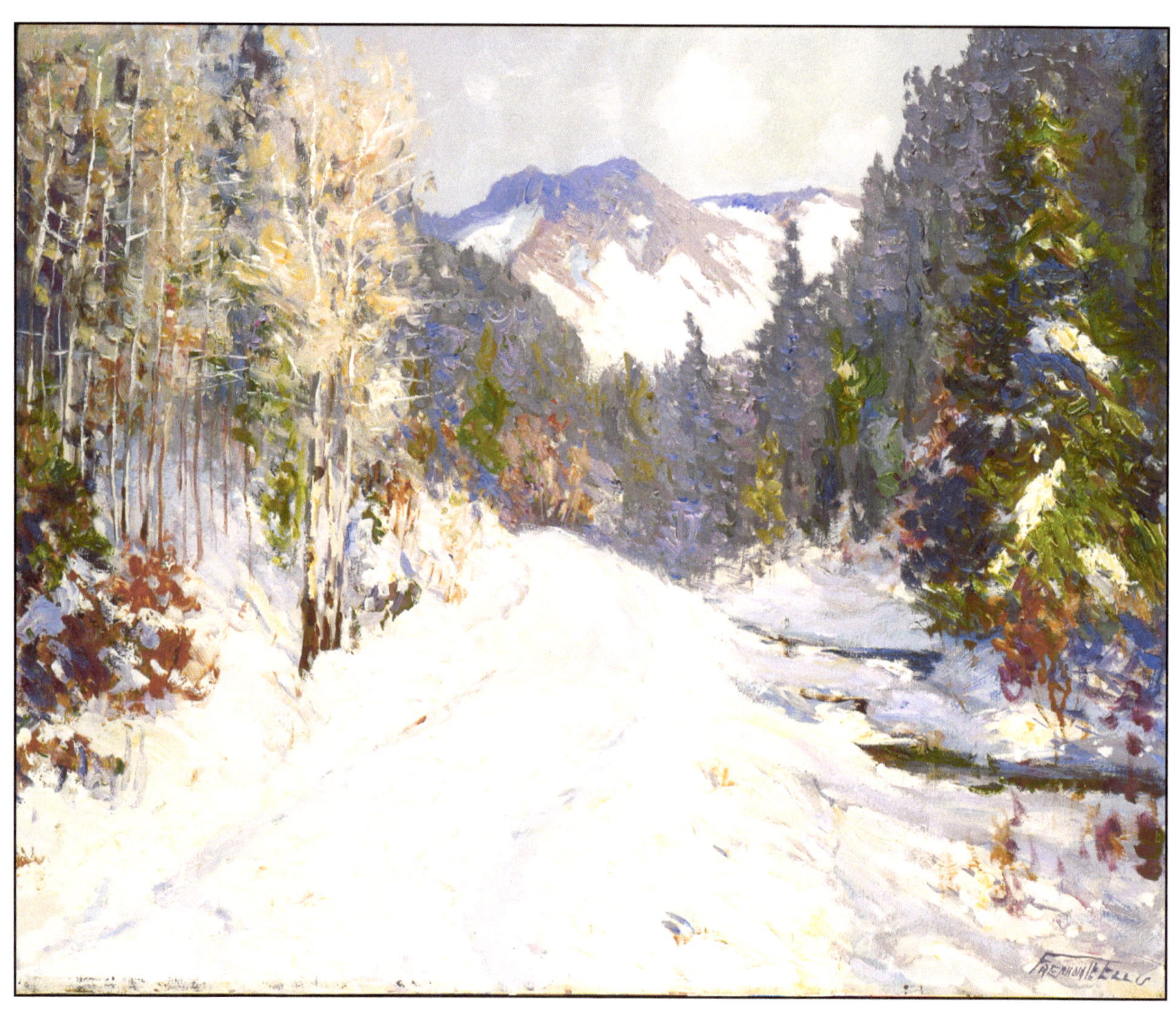

Winter, Cumbres Pass, oil on canvas, 20 x 25 inches.
Collection of the Stark Museum of Art, Orange, Texas. 31.20/78.

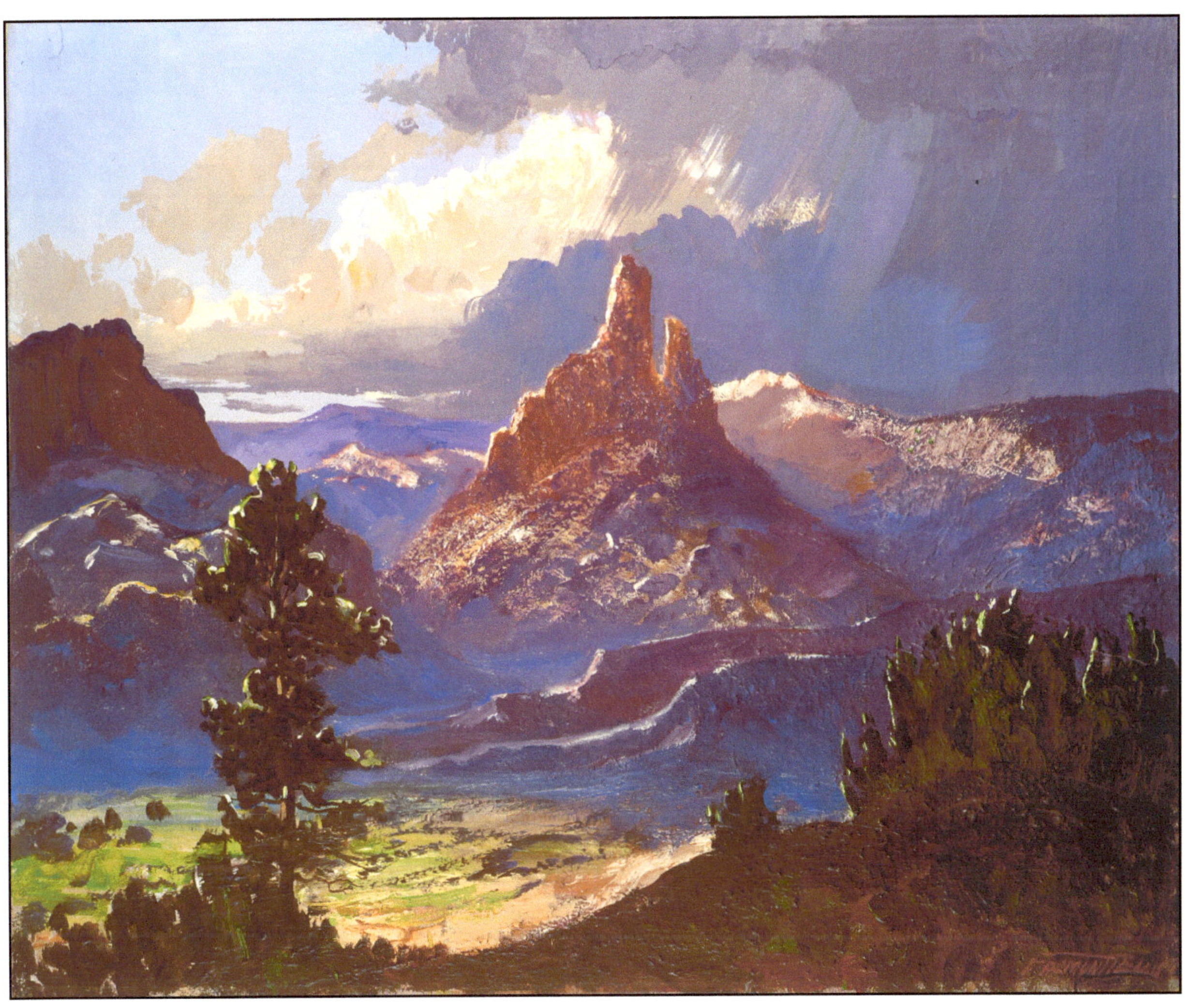

Navajo Canyon, oil on canvas, 24 x 30 inches.
Collection of Stark Museum of Art, Orange, Texas. 31.20/8.

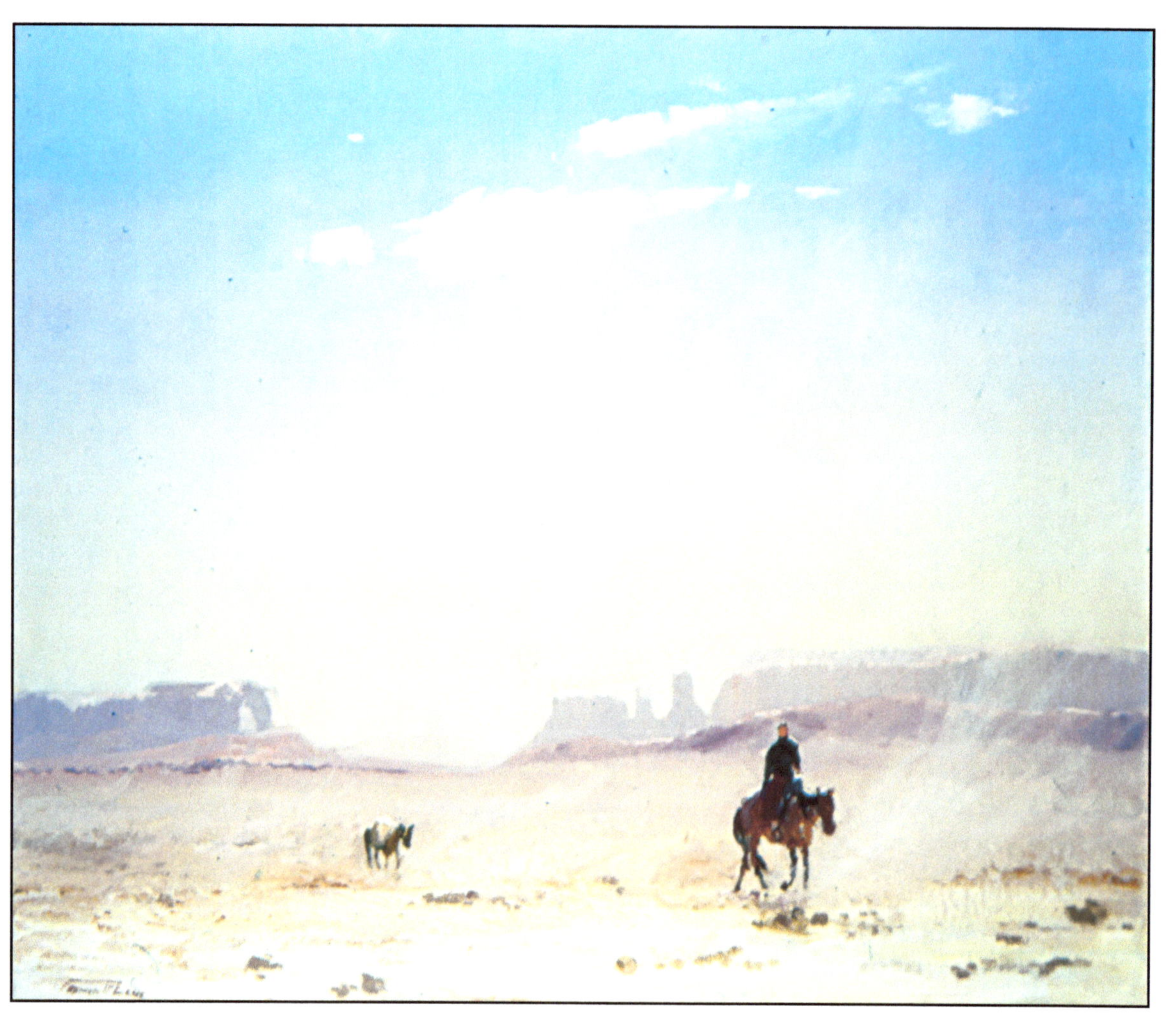

Blowing Sand, oil on canvasboard, 25 x 30 inches.
Collection of the Stark Museum of Art, Orange, Texas. 31.20/7.

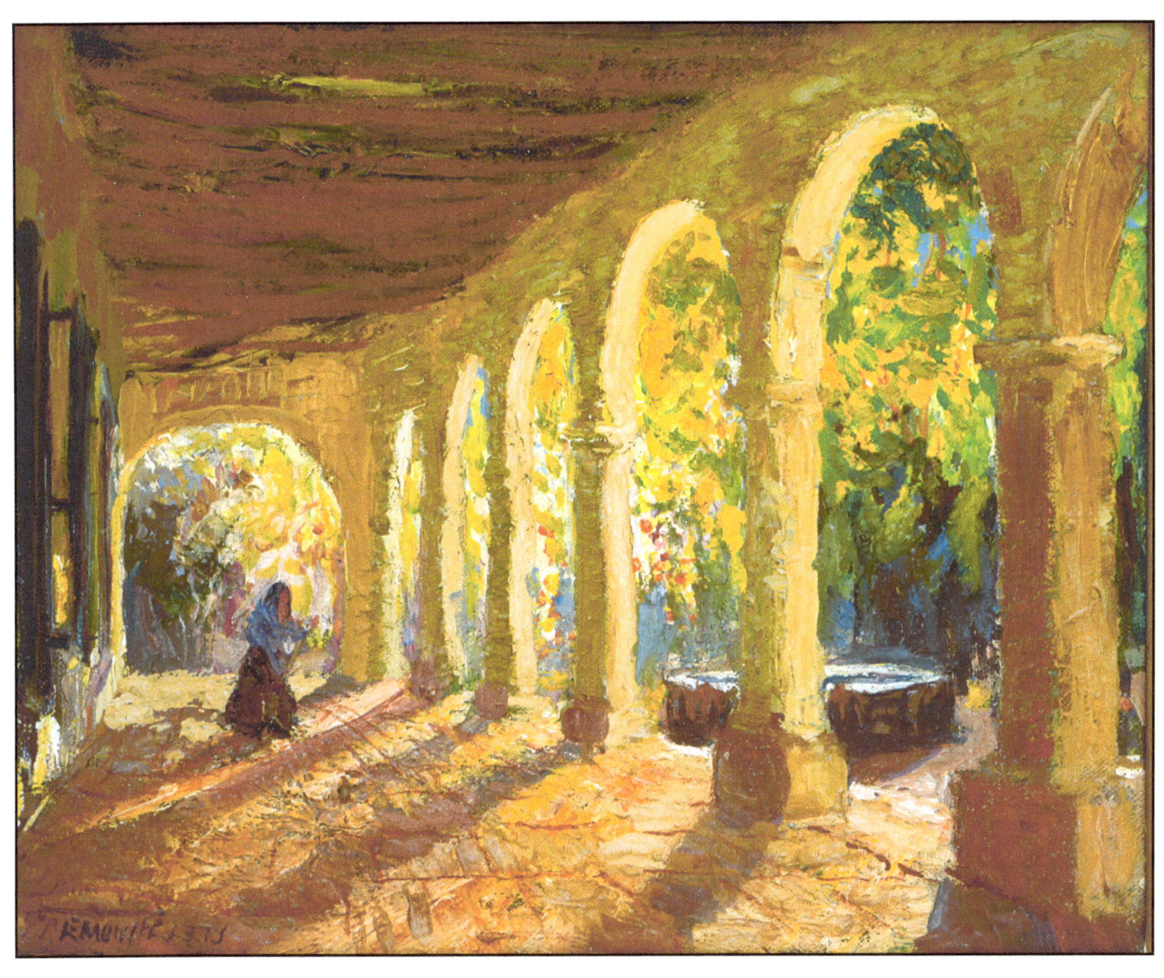

Mexican Woman, oil on canvas, 10 7/8 x 13 3/4 inches.
Collection of the Stark Museum of Art. Orange, Texas 31.20/1.

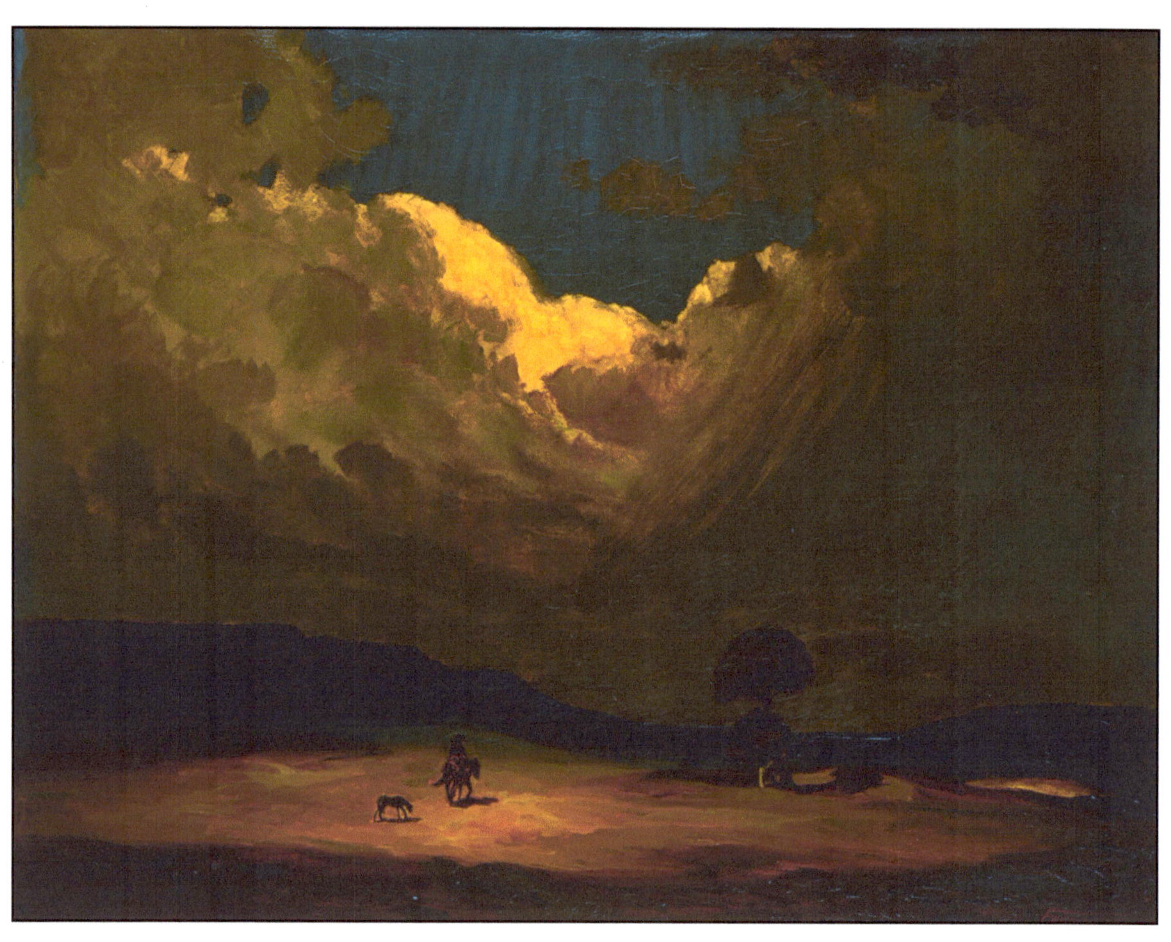

The Storm, oil on canvas, 30 x 40 inches.
Collection of the Stark Museum of Art, Orange, Texas.
Painting inspired by music entitled *The Steppes*, sung by a Russian opera singer. 31 20/30.

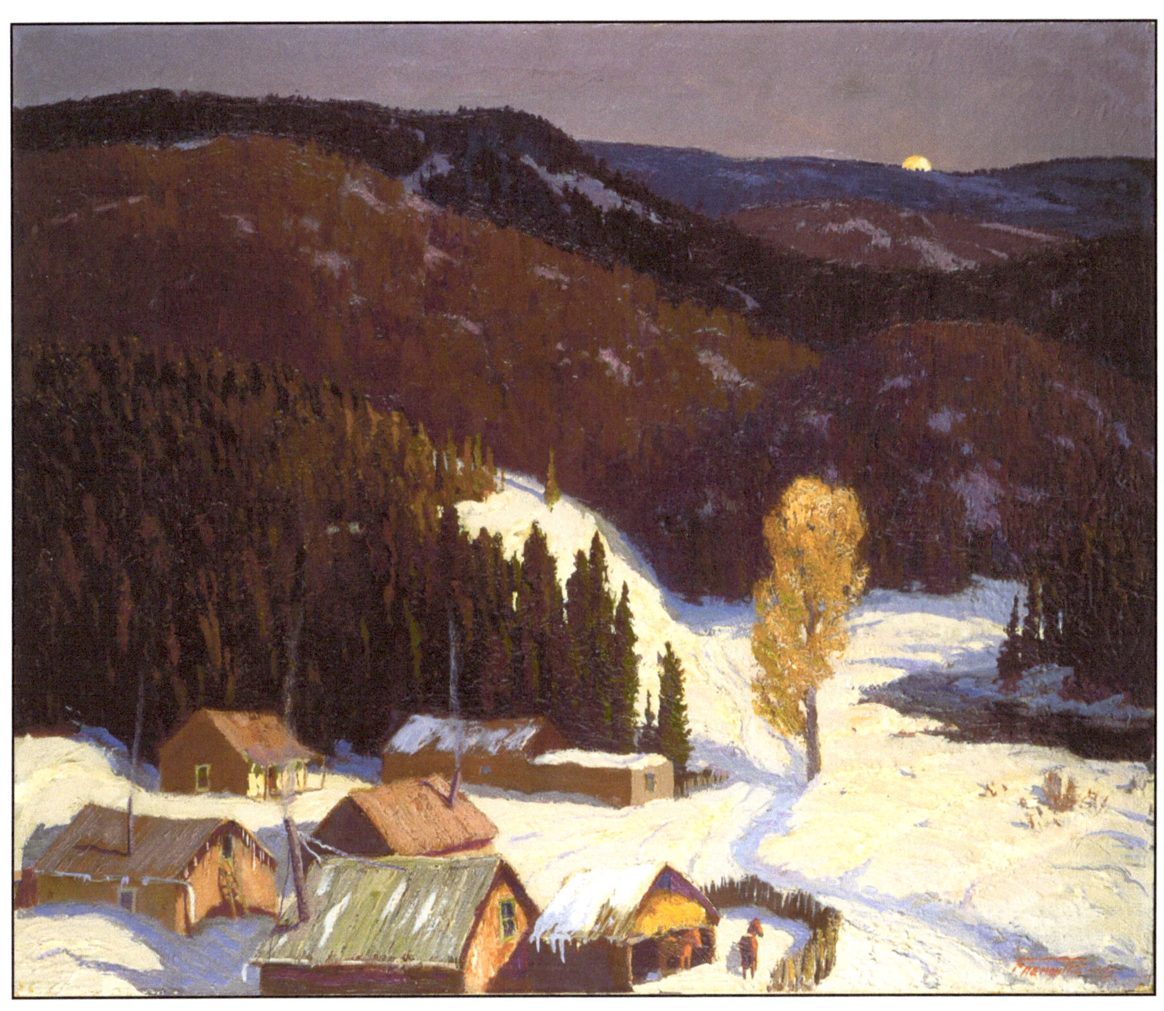

Winter Evening, oil on canvas, 29 x 36 inches.
Collection of the Stark Museum of Art, Orange, Texas. 31.20/24.

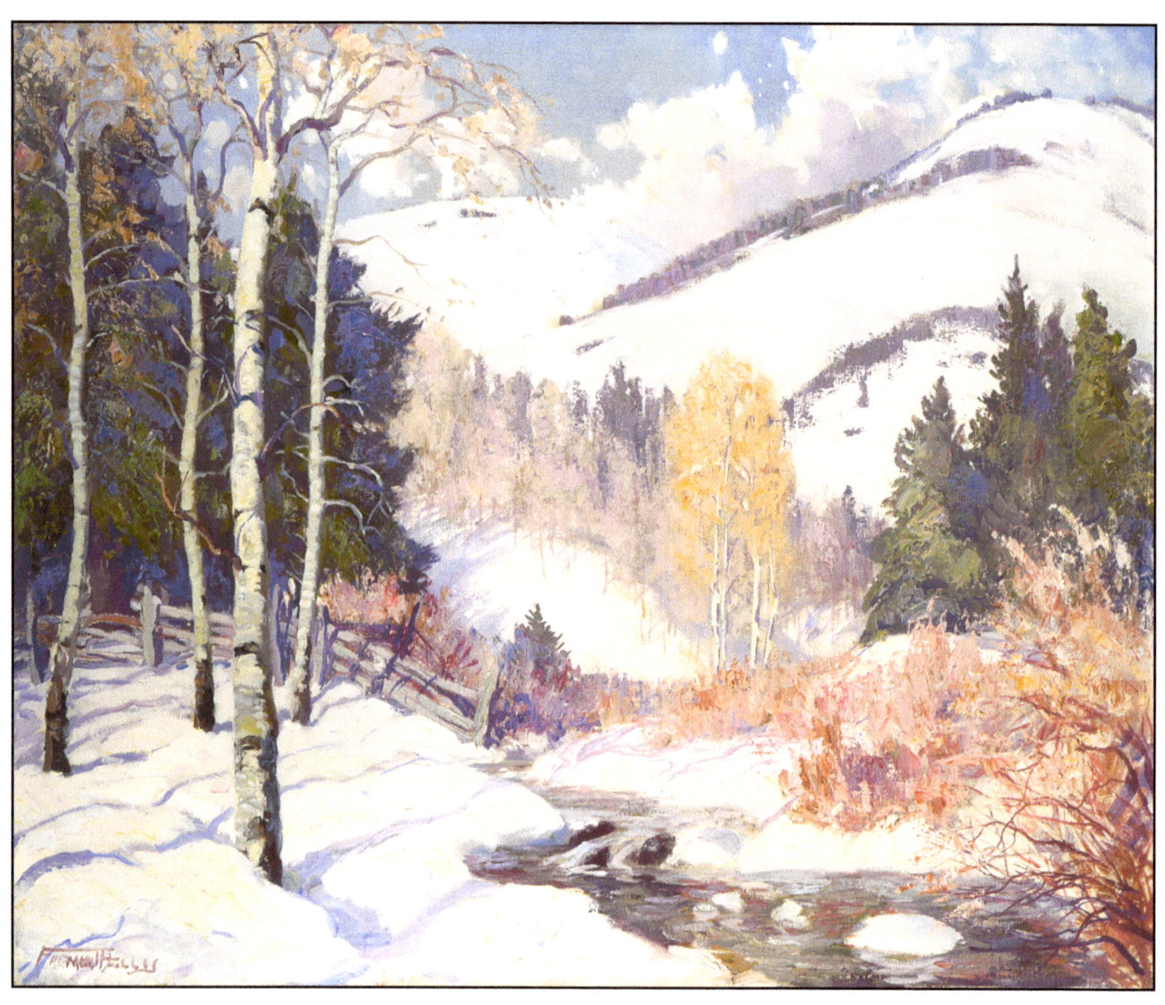

Winter, Glorieta, oil on canvas, 24 x 30 inches.
Collection of the Stark Museum of Art, Orange, Texas. 31.20/9.

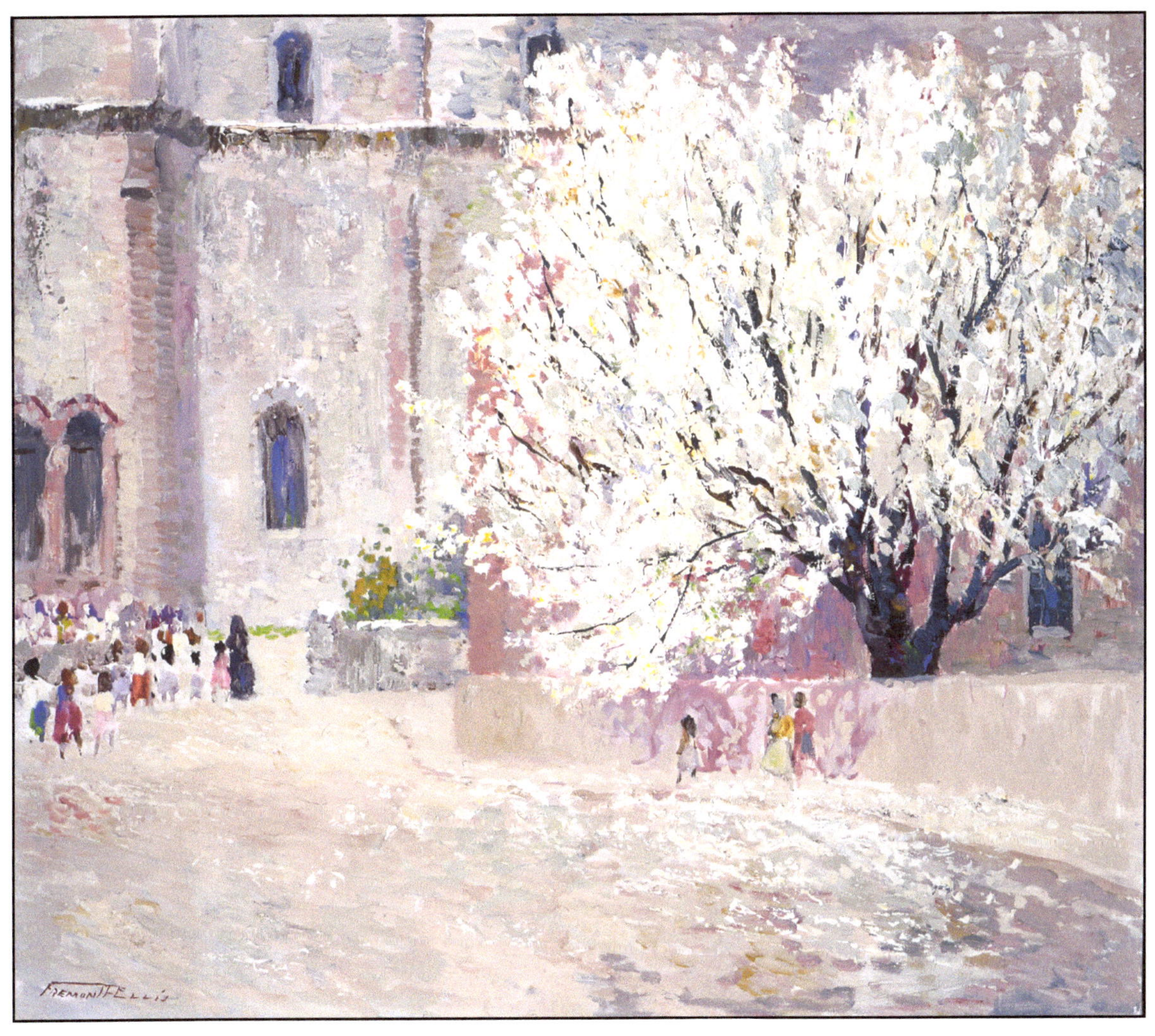

The Almond Tree, c. 1950, oil on wood, 25 x 30 inches.
Collection of the Stark Museum of Art, Orange, Texas 31.20/6.

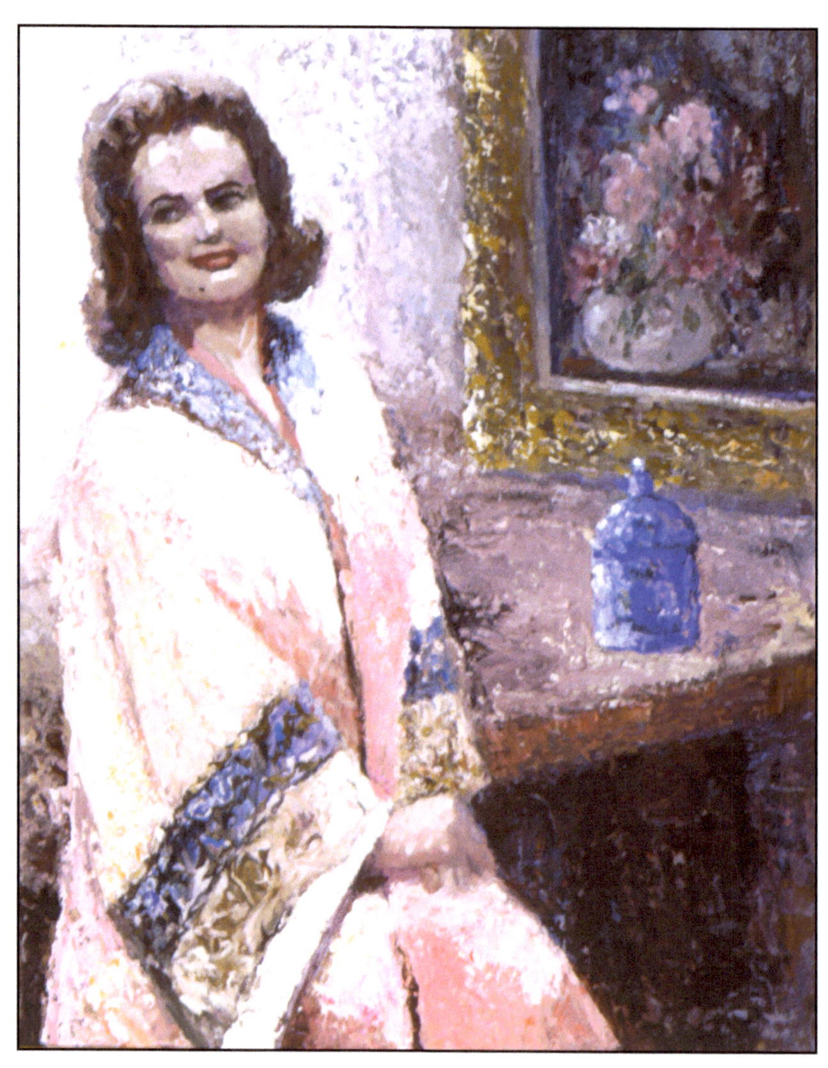

Bambi in Robe, circa 1950, oil on canvas, 32 x 26 inches.
Collection of the New Mexico Museum of Art, Santa Fe, New Mexico.
Gift of Bambi Ellis, 1995.

11

STUDIO ON CANYON ROAD

The 1940s decade was a busy and productive era for the Ellis family. Fremont's art was well known now and in demand, and he painted consistently every day. Lencha took her daughter to Mexico City and enrolled her in a business course and also arranged for her to study dance under Pepe Antin, Carmen Amaya's partner. Both Lencha and Fremont spent time in Mexico frequently checking on their daughter and visiting with friends. Their son, Fred, was now in the United States Navy.

After Bambi finished her schooling, the Ellises continued a yearly trip to Mexico. They rented the home of Jose Mojica, a famous Mexican opera singer. Mojica had retired from the opera and entered a monastery. Fremont found renewed artistic energy in painting the Mexican landscapes.

Ellis' art was attracting even more attention in the 1950s, and he won the Hazel Hyde Morrison Prize and Bronze Medal from the Oakland Museum in California. His paintings were in demand all over the Southwest in museums for public collections. In 1956 he was given the Merit Award by the Springville Museum in Springville, Utah.

Lutcher Stark, a wealthy entrepreneur who established the Stark Museum of Art in Orange Texas, made frequent trips to Santa Fe. He was a great friend and admirer of Fremont Ellis and his work and bought many of his paintings to put on display in a permanent collection in his art museum. The Stark Museum still has the largest collection of Fremont Ellis paintings.

In 1955 Fremont made the decision that he should have a studio in Santa Fe where he and his works would be more accessible to the general public. His logical choice for location was on Canyon Road where other artists had started to build studios when *Los Cinco Pintores* built studios on the adjacent Camino del Monte Sol. Lencha did not agree with this proposed change. She loved the ranch and wanted to stay there so Fremont followed through with his plan and rented a studio on Canyon Road. Shortly after that he bought a home and studio on Canyon Road which had been designed by fellow artist, William Penhallow Henderson. It remains to this day one of the most beautiful and unusual adobe buildings in the city.

Lencha never joined Fremont in the home on Canyon Road. Her health was not good, and the sadness she experienced over Fremont's move back to Santa Fe may have shortened her life. She passed away four years later on October 12, 1959, from advanced complications of diabetes. Fremont was inconsolable over the death of his wife.

Fremont Ellis never remarried, and he spent the latter part of his life in the beautiful residence and studio he had bought on historic Canyon Road in Santa Fe, New Mexico. This two story residence where Ellis lived until his death in 1985 has been Federally designated as a unique historical property.

A feeling of serenity must have enveloped those visiting Fremont Ellis' house during those years as they entered the two-storied balconied living room-studio filled with natural light. The terra cotta tile floor was covered with soft-hued oriental rugs which complemented many fine examples of Southwestern furniture designed and built by Henderson which enhanced Ellis' own light-filled paintings on the white-washed adobe walls.

The high thick outside walls guaranteed Ellis the privacy and peace he required to produce his best work. The upstairs balcony adjoined two bedroom suites, a bathroom, and a sitting room filled with books. The artist called it his library where he relaxed and enjoyed his reading. A guest bedroom, bath, studio, kitchen, and large enclosed patio completed the downstairs.

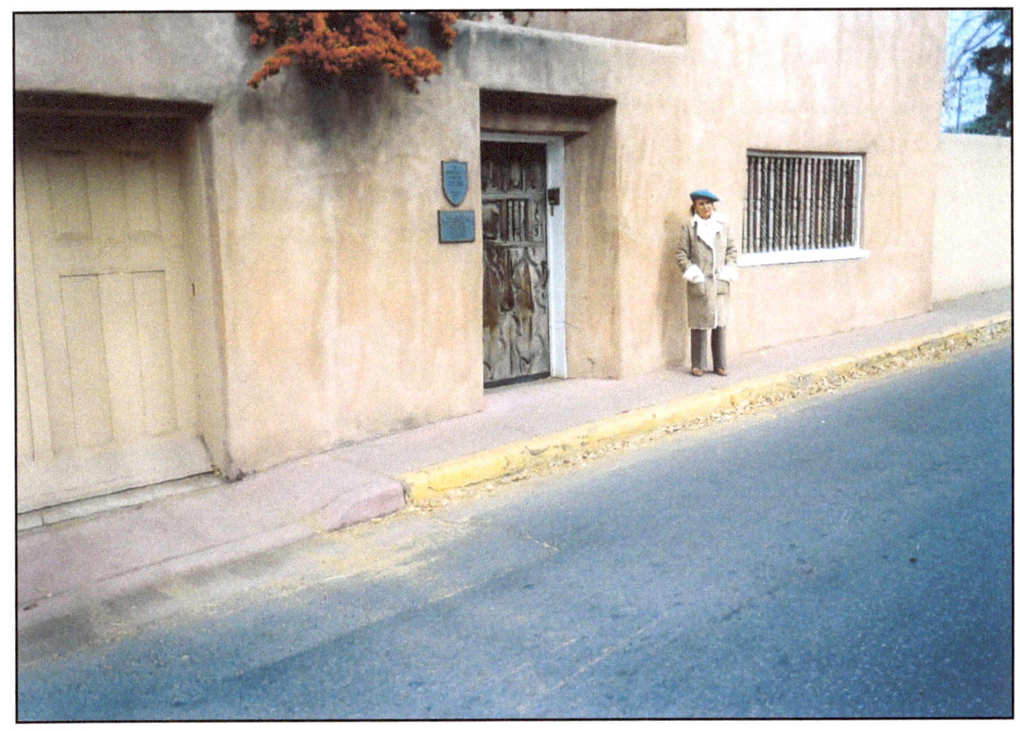

Bambi Ellis stands in front of her father's last residence and studio on Canyon Road in Santa Fe, New Mexico. Photograph by Barbara Foster.

Ellis painted at a towering easel which added a dramatic note to the living room and furniture. It pleased Ellis to paint in this setting. "I like to see how my pictures look in that surrounding because that's where they'll hang," he said. He often looked down from the balcony to get a distant view of the painting in progress.

There was also a downstairs studio viewing room where the walls were hung with his paintings while others were stacked against the wall on the floor.

Ellis favored the same carved, lightly-brushed-with-gold frames the Impressionists had used. He would put a picture into a frame soon after starting it because, he said, "When a picture is in a frame, you can judge how far to take it. If it's unframed, you can take it too far."

Fremont Ellis was very particular about the frames he used. His first frames were hand made by his close friend, Earl Stone. Later, Raymond Jonson, who taught art at the University of New Mexico and was also an abstract painter and framer, made his frames. Later he got frames from the Louvre Framing Company in Chicago until they went out of business. They would send him samples of the frames they had available, and he would choose the right frame for each painting. Then later, he purchased frames from the Heidenrijck Framing Company in New York City, the company that had originally made frames for Rembrandt many years earlier in Holland.

Ellis' painting was his life. He commented once to his daughter, "I know I would be completely lost if I didn't paint." He was able to continue painting until shortly before his death at the age of 87 years. If he had to run errands in town for most of the day and not get home until late in the afternoon, he would immediately go to his easel and "fool around a little bit with painting," as he expressed it, "or I feel like I have wasted the whole day. I don't think I'd live without painting."

During this time, Ellis improved his skills as a businessman and found increasing success in being able to market his paintings with the assistance of his daughter, Bambi. In addition to his affection for his home and studio, he became a Studebaker car admirer, and in 1963 he bought an Avanti. A few years later he traded this car, plus one of his paintings to Ray Altman, the brother of Avanti Motors' founder, Nate Altman, for a 1967 Avanti 11. The *Avanti Magazine* in its fall/winter issue of 2001 had this to say about Ellis. "He knew what many Avanti owners share and feel whenever they drive their car—that it is a rolling work of art."

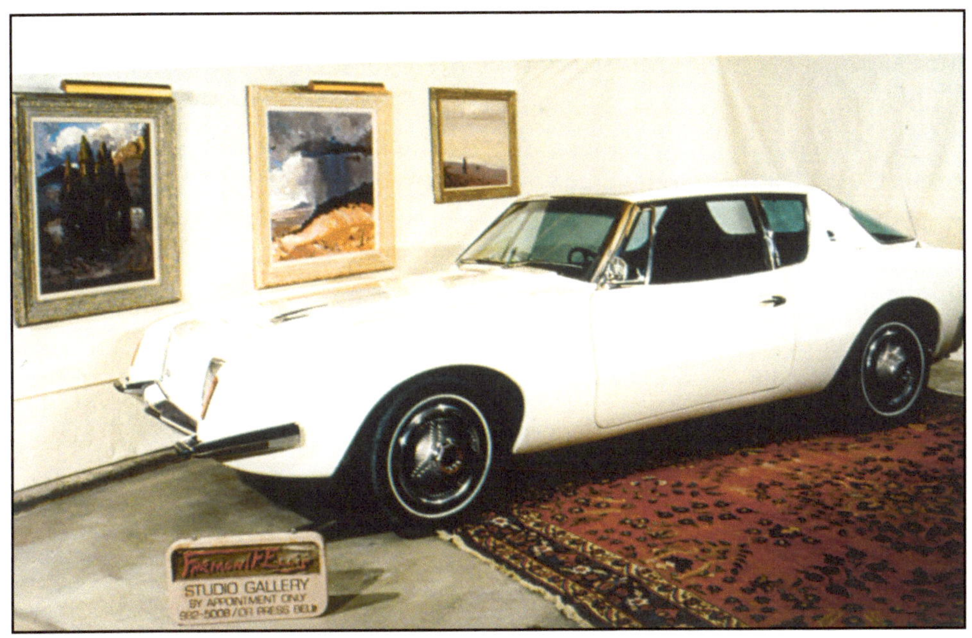

Fremont Ellis showing off his Avanti with some of his paintings in the background. Photograph courtesy of Bambi Ellis.

After having received the Governor's Award for Excellence in the Arts in 1974, each succeeding governor has been allowed to choose one of the Ellis paintings from the New Mexico Museum of Art to be hung in the governor's mansion. The *Canyon de Chelly* painting which was set in Navajo Country has been the painting of choice for most of the governors. It now hangs in a small intimate sitting room, and the deep rusts of the coral cliffs and turquoise blues in the mountains and sky match the same hues in the carpet and vases and pillows. The room is decorated in the Southwestern style. The Navajo woman and patch of green field and blue thread of river that runs by a *hogan* are all dwarfed by the vastness of the huge coral cliffs. As usual in his paintings, Mother Nature is emphasized, and the human element downplayed.

Fremont Ellis had long wished to go back and visit the place of his birth, Virginia City, Montana, so he made a trip to the Northwest in 1980. He marveled at the rough wooden building where he had drawn his first breath and which still stands on the main street of this old gold mining town. He also visited the little hamlet of Pony, and then journeyed to Missoula, Montana's western city of culture and education. He paused briefly in Hamilton, Montana, remembering his first year of school.

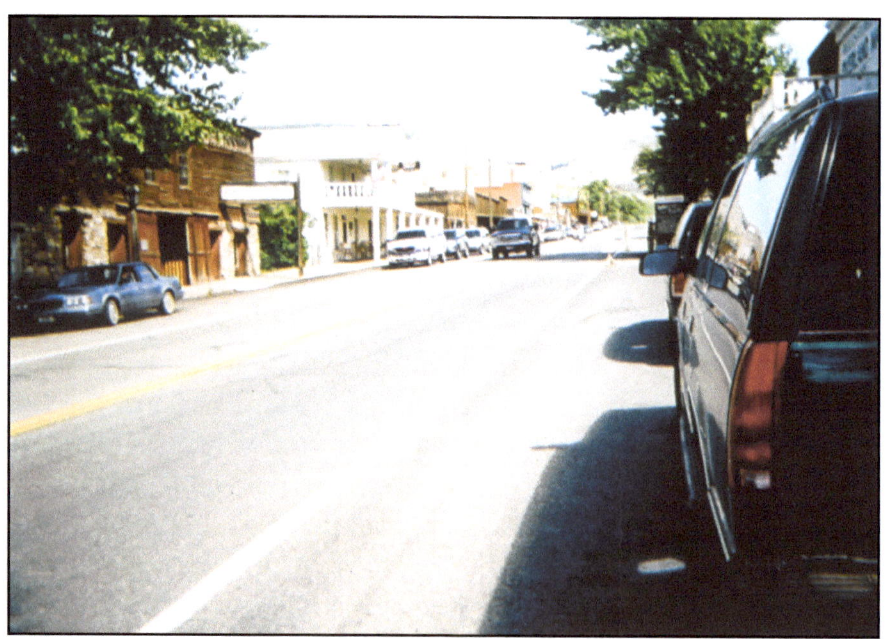

Main Street of Virginia City, Montana, as it looks today. Photograph by Frances Jones.

When he returned to Santa Fe, Fremont later described his trip back to the northwestern country of his early life and told his daughter how much he loved the "Big Sky Country of Montana." "I'd move up there," he stated, "if it wasn't so damned cold."

Fremont Ellis died January 12, 1985, in his eighty-seventh year as the result of an injury received in a car accident and a series of bad falls. Fremont and Lencha are buried in the Rosario Cemetery in Santa Fe next to Archbishop Lamy's crypt.

Not long before he died, Fremont Ellis commented when asked what he thought made his painting good, "The thing that really makes a picture good—you can't tell."

He was unassuming about his work to the end.

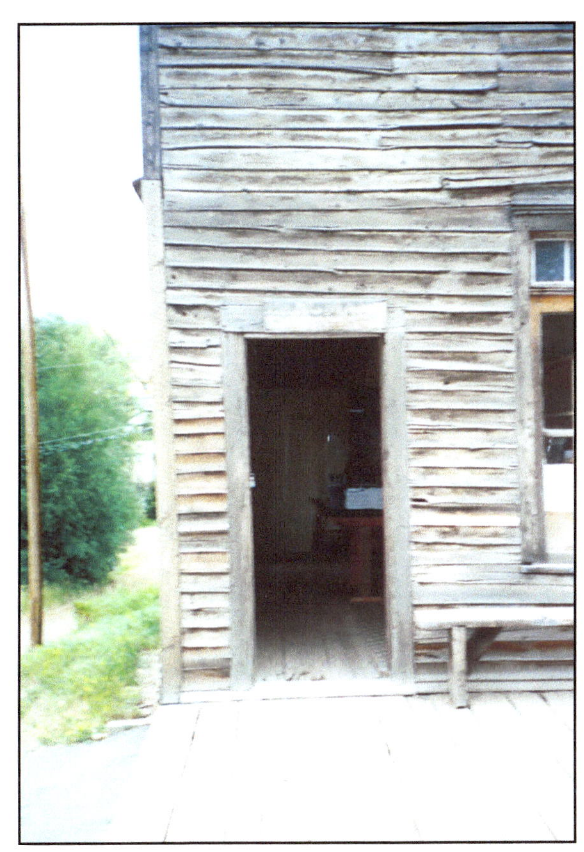

The building in Virginia City, Montana, where Fremont Ellis was born, as it looks today. Photograph by Barbara Foster.

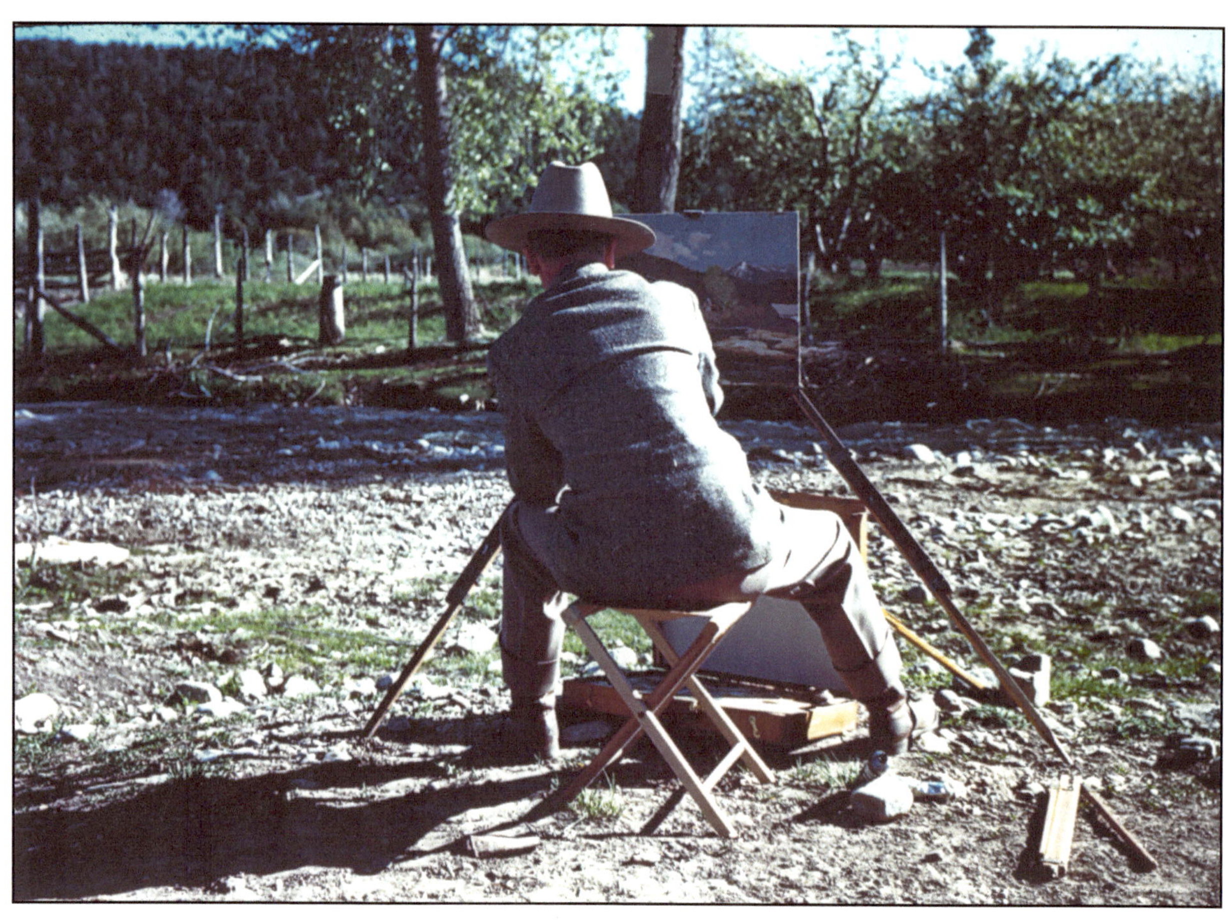

Fremont Ellis working on some outdoor sketching.

12

PHILOSOPHY and PAINTING STYLE

Ellis once said of his more than two thousand paintings, "I have no method. If a musician plays by ear, then I paint by eye. What is to be painted determines how it is to be painted." He became known as the Aspen Painter because of his beautiful aspen works. This description was a compliment to him, but at the same time he resented it. He didn't want to be categorized as only one type of painter. "I paint many things," he would say, "as well as many kinds of trees." Indeed, the aspens in many of his paintings, such as *Aspen Time Picnickers,* were breathtaking, but so were the majestic firs and magnificent cottonwoods and flowering fruit trees in other paintings.

But most art critics agreed that whether he painted a tree or a lake or a mountain or a valley or a sky or a desert or an ocean, nature was the dominating theme of his paintings. The people or animals in them were incidental and insignificant in comparison to the strength and magnificence of nature that his paintings emphasized so dramatically.

He said very late in his life, "I'm still a student. It's still a puzzle to me. Values, color relation, vibration of colors—it's really a complicated process, at least to me. When I first came to Santa Fe, I looked at the works of some of the old painters and said, 'In five years I'll be doing that.' Now I keep pushing that time schedule back another five years. And I'm still trying."

Each painting, whether the scene portrays his "white light" of the Southwest (as he called it) on shimmering, golden mountain aspens or the contrast of a shadowed mountain with back lit clouds, the sweep of the sky in desert country or a peaceful view of the sea shore, all are breath-taking to everyone but the artist who felt he must continually strive to reach perfection "which just might be possible in another five years."

Over the years Ellis admitted to having changed techniques to express his subject, but he insisted he had no system at all and no methods. He has been quoted as saying, "If you ask me how to mix a certain color, I couldn't tell you. It's just intuitive. Oh, I have distinct ideas about how to go about painting. Get the composition laid in and half the battle is won. I paint all over the canvas, fill it with beautiful shapes, getting the large masses arranged."

Fremont Ellis found in Santa Fe the contacts, the inspiration, and the atmosphere he sought and set himself to the vigorous task of reproducing New Mexico's landscape while he emphasized at all times the unique shimmering light which so enthralled him, and which he detected in the southwestern beauty. The light in the Albert Bierstadt paintings he had first viewed in the Metropolitan Museum of Art in New York City had been the most intriguing part of this artist's works to the young boy. "How does he put that light in there?" he had asked in awe. This light element he concentrated on so effectively the rest of his painting career in his scenes of the caminos, arroyos, adobes, mountains, and people of New Mexico.

Ellis explained his intrigue with light to Jill Warren, a writer for *New Mexico Magazine:* "Light changes so quickly it's impossible to capture it by setting one's easel up and painting directly from life. I strive to catch the mood of a certain place on a certain day by using my mind's eye for the vision and my feelings for the mood after I am back in the studio." He felt that others could then get from the painting what he saw and felt at the time he was relating to the natural scene and could then conjure up in themselves similar feelings.

Sandra Koops wrote in *The New Mexican* in 1975 the following description of Ellis' work:

> The use of light and shadows in his work is true. If someone were to look out across the land an hour or so before sunset on a very clear day, the qualities of the sun on the tops of trees, on the slopes of rocks, indeed, on whole faces of mountains, the clarity of undiluted gold light is what he would see, and it is just exactly that quality that Ellis has put on his canvases. Though he uses a heavy stroke, seeming almost as if a palette knife had been used and not a brush at all, the sense of light is undeniably there. Many of his works show him as an idealist, a romanticist, and his *Landscape with Road and Trees* shows a Van Gogh bent.

Critic Robert Bright, stated in *The New Mexican,* "Mr. Ellis has the rare gift of being able to paint not merely what he sees before his eyes, but what he experiences from inside, and he has chosen for his purpose the medium of impressionism—and because it is the way he feels things, his impressionism is romantic."

Ellis had a strong desire to learn and perfect throughout his life. He read profusely when he was not painting. He liked to read biographies of painters and John Twachtman was an artist to whom he especially related. He read his biography by Eliot Clark and underlined meaningful passages such as: "Naturalistic accuracy of detail is subordinated to more universal relations, and the impression is produced by suggestion rather than by objective delineation." The pages containing the passages in this book which were especially meaningful to him, he marked with small pieces of paper.

Fremont Ellis zealously read anything C. Edgar Payne, a California artist whom he much admired, wrote. From *Composition of Outdoor Painting,* he underlined this quote: "Individuality in thought, respect for nature and established truths and principles combine to make the road that can lead to true original artistic expression. There may be other means, but they have not been found, and it is doubtful if they ever will." Ellis built his painting career upon these truths, and especially urged younger painters to figure out their individual painting style rather than to copy the old masters.

Ellis often quoted Sir Joshua Reynolds who wrote, "The eye sees no more than it knows, and we take no more from the world than we take into it. Accordingly, we discern the finer characteristics. We must ourselves reach a degree of refinements, or we shall fail to recognize it in others." Ellis worked for that degree of refinement in all areas of his life—his constant search for broadening his mind, his striving for perfection in his painting, and his words and looks in everyday life. He articulated on a deeper level than the average person, and he took care of the physical needs of his body with temperance and reasonableness. He dressed and spoke like a country gentleman. However, he never "put on airs" and pretended to be anything but what he was. "I'm just a common man with the likes and dislikes of most people. That's why my painting strikes a chord with so many people."

In the front of Ellis' sketchbook he wrote some of his inner thoughts about painting. He explained, "Instead of trying to imitate exactly what I see before my eyes, I am using color in a much more arbitrary way in order to express myself more strongly. I believe I have been somewhat successful in attempting to capture and recreate the rhythmic vitality of nature."

Ellis also wrote a paragraph of negative criticism about his work. "I have worked over paintings too much and too long. I simply must overcome this habit of changing and changing, making constant alterations because the result is a final painting that has no resemblance to the first version or impression."

Ellis' love affair with impressionistic painting started early in his career. When asked why he painted the Ranchos de Taos Church in 1930, he replied, "I have always loved churches. But the thing that impressed me about Ranchos de Taos was not so much the church itself, but the setting and the background. I painted the subject as I felt about it. It's the impression; that's what I want to paint."

Fremont Ellis loved music, and one of his best paintings was inspired by the soundtrack of the movie, *The Heartbeat,* a French film. Ellis' daughter, Bambi, gave him the music sound track of the movie. Sometime later he invited her into his studio, and to the notes from the sound track, he unveiled the painting he had been inspired to create as he listened to the music. Bambi still has this painting, titled *By the Sea*, in her living room (in 2006), and she counts it as one of her most treasured possessions.

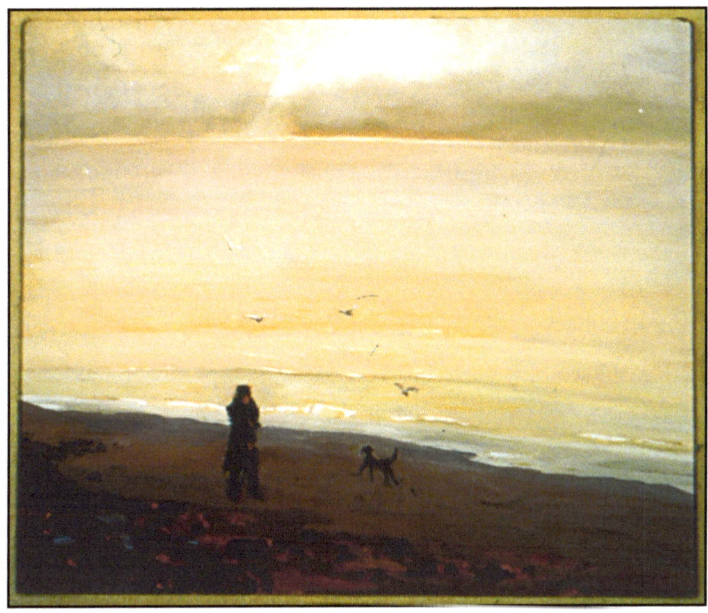

By the Sea. Ellis painted this picture for his daughter, Bambi, as he listened to the sound track of the movie, *Heartbreak.* 23 x 30 inches, oil on canvas. Photograph courtesy of Bambi Ellis.

The somber colors of the sand and the ocean waves in this painting are not softened by the heavy dreary atmosphere. In the movie a young man and woman had met on the beach, fallen in love, married, and lived a long happily married life near the beach. After her death, the broken hearted spouse walked the beach nightly with his departed's dog, reminiscing about the wonderful love they had shared. So, the lack of light which played such an integral part in Ellis' paintings gives this painting the dramatic solemnity and feeling of loss he wished to impart. This painting is evidence as to the correctness of Fremont Ellis' reputation as one of America's most renowned romantic and emotional painters.

In summary, one can correctly state that Ellis' paintings are strongly impressionistic in feeling, marked by heightened emotionalism, and sometimes portraying a tendency toward gloom. When one of his paintings just missed winning a prize in an important California art show, his father wrote him, commenting that he had submitted a good painting which had caused much favorable comment, but he wanted to know why he had painted something so dark and depressing. But, there were the times in the artist's life when he suffered from depression. Perhaps this painting was a result of innermost despairing feelings at the time.

Unlike some of his fellow artists, Ellis did not decry the abstractionists. He felt that a good abstract painting must have the same quality as a good representational painting. He would often reflect, "The overall effect is the same; if the painting is good, it means something to the person who looks at it." Ellis always tried to stimulate in young artists the search for original thinking and creating. He, himself, had been influenced by impressionist painters, but he urged young painters to search for their own style and have the courage to follow their own thinking. This painter of natural talent did whatever seemed appropriate to him naturally. And, as an admirer of Claude Monet and Edouard Manet, he painted natural scenes from memory to capture the aura of a mood as he followed the techniques of these old masters, and he became renowned as one of America's most romantic and emotional painters. His paintings eliminated detail in favor of an overall generalized treatment of subject matter.

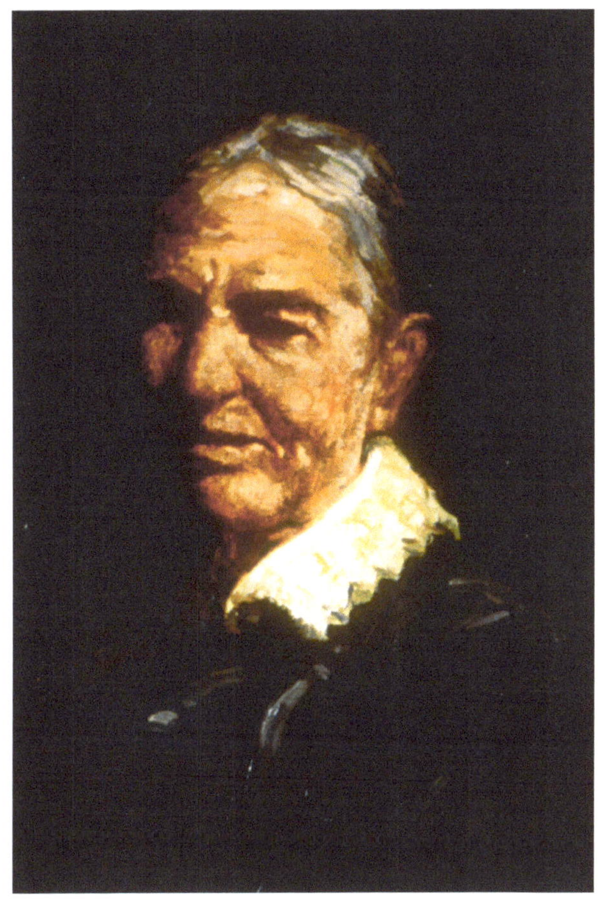

The mother of Laurencita Gonzales de Ellis. The style of this painting shows the influence of Rembrandt. He did this painting from memory. His mother-in-law would not sit for him to paint her portrait. Photograph courtesy of Bambi Ellis.

Ellis' brushwork was as vigorous and definite as he seemed to be with life itself. In an Ellis painting there are often broad areas of tactile pigment. He loved the physical act of laying down stroke after stroke of rich color, layer over layer, thus building up paint. "Paint can have a wonderful quality that attracts you in itself," he often said.

But he was never satisfied with his accomplishments and never wanted to hear or read tributes to his artistic genius. He remained to the end a modest, unassuming painter who strove to perfect his work. He never quit working on a painting until it was sold. As long as it stayed in his studio, he would work on it.

"Sometimes I'd come to my studio in the morning and swear someone had been in there messing up my paintings," he would say. "I would immediately see a problem area in one of them and go to work to fix it."

Being the perfectionist that he was, Fremont Ellis probably underestimated his painting. In later years when he received many awards, he refused to accept them in person. His daughter, Bambi, always represented her father at these events.

From *Works and Words of Santa Fe Artists,* a C. R. Wenzell Publication in Santa Fe, Fremont Ellis said, "This I know. In the final analysis, what gives to a work of art its distinction are the intangibles; the undefinable, the unexplainable qualities that can only be sensed or felt."

AWARDS

Huntington Award, LA County Museum of Art, 1924
Hazel Hyde Morrison Prize & Bronze Medal, Oakland Museum, 1956
Merit Award (twice), Springville museum, Springville, UT, 1956
Governor's Award for Excellence in the Arts, Santa Fe, 1974
Gold Medal, National Cowboy Hall of Fame, National Academy of Western Art, Oklahoma City, 1981
Artist's Award of Honor, Rosary International, Santa Fe, 1983
Distinguished Artist Award, *New Mexico Magazine*, Santa Fe, 1985

PUBLIC COLLECTIONS

Anschutz Collection, Denver, Colorado
El Paso Museum of Art, El Paso, TX
Gilcrease Institute of American History and Art, Tulsa, OK
Los Angeles County Museum of Art, Los Angeles, CA
Museum of Art, Springville, UT
Museum of Fine Arts, Santa Fe, NM
Philbrook Art Center, Tulsa, OK
Roswell Museum and Art Center Roswell, NM
Santa Fe Railroad Collection
Stark Museum of Art, Orange, TX
Texas Tech University Museum, Lubbock, TX
The White House, Permanent Collection, Washington, DC

LATER PAINTINGS of FREMONT F. ELLIS

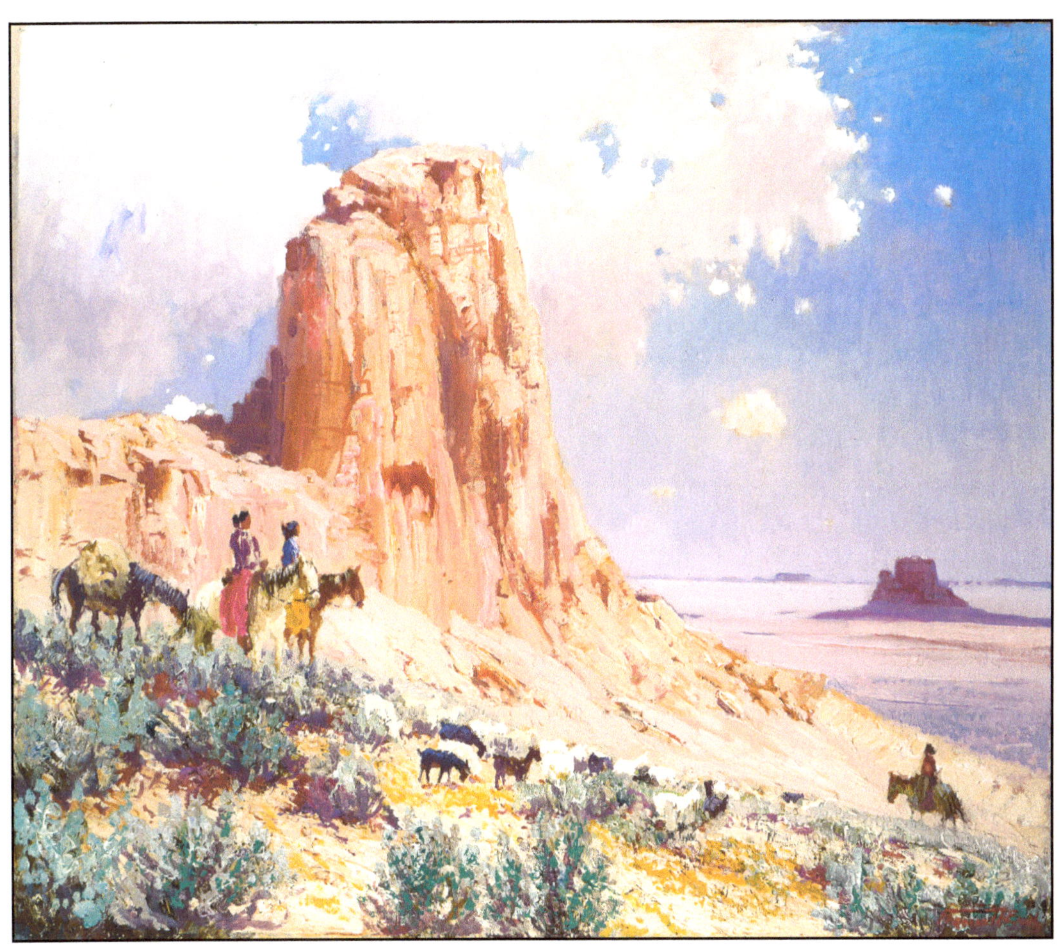

The Red Rock, oil on board, 24 7/8 x 30 inches.
Collection of Stark Museum of Art, Orange, Texas.

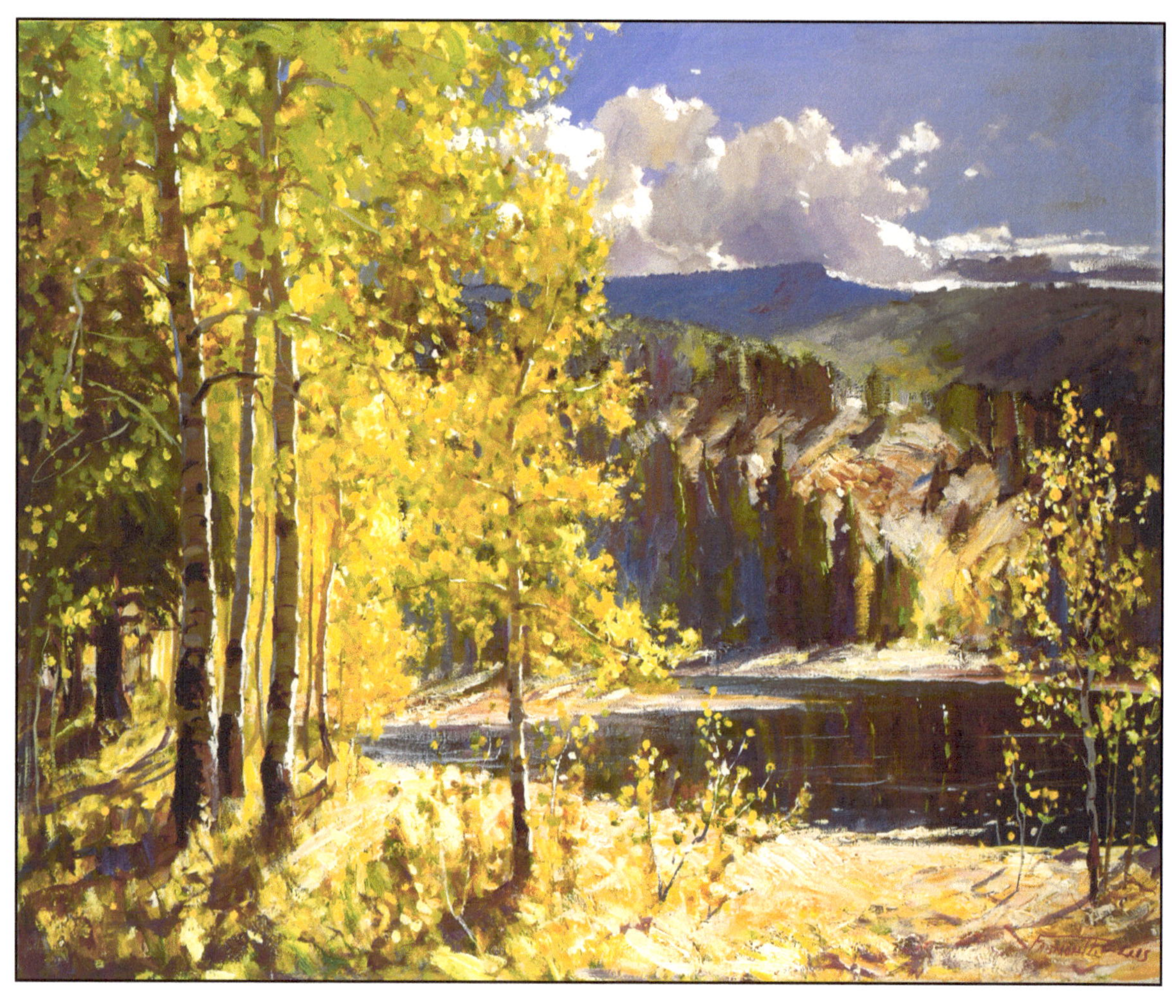

Mountain Lake, oil on canvas, 24 1/8 x 30 1/8 inches.
Collection of Stark Museum of Art, Orange, Texas. Mountain Lake.

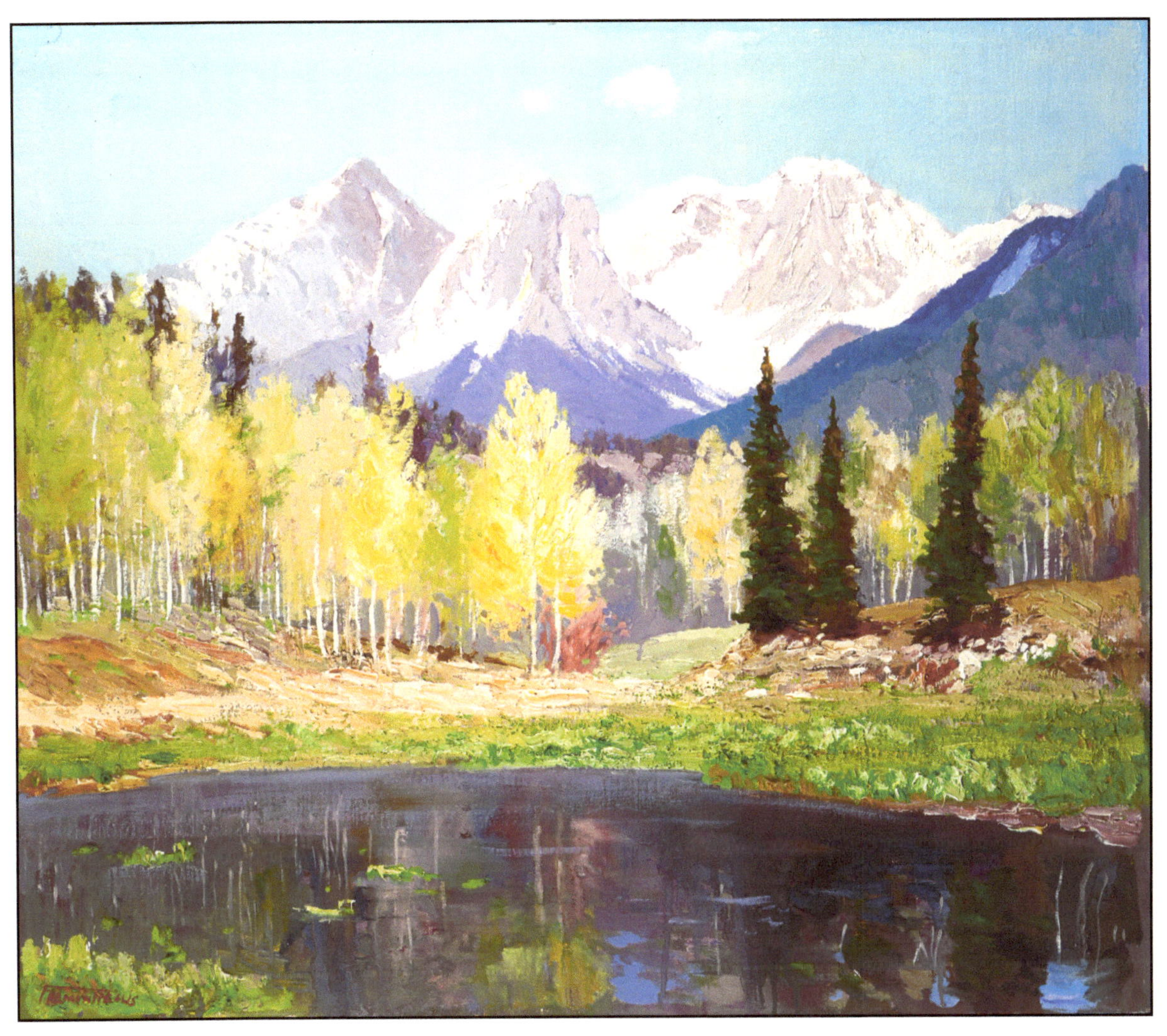

Spring in the High Country, oil on canvasboard, 24 7/8 x 30 1/8 inches.
Collection of Stark Museum of Art, Orange, Texas.

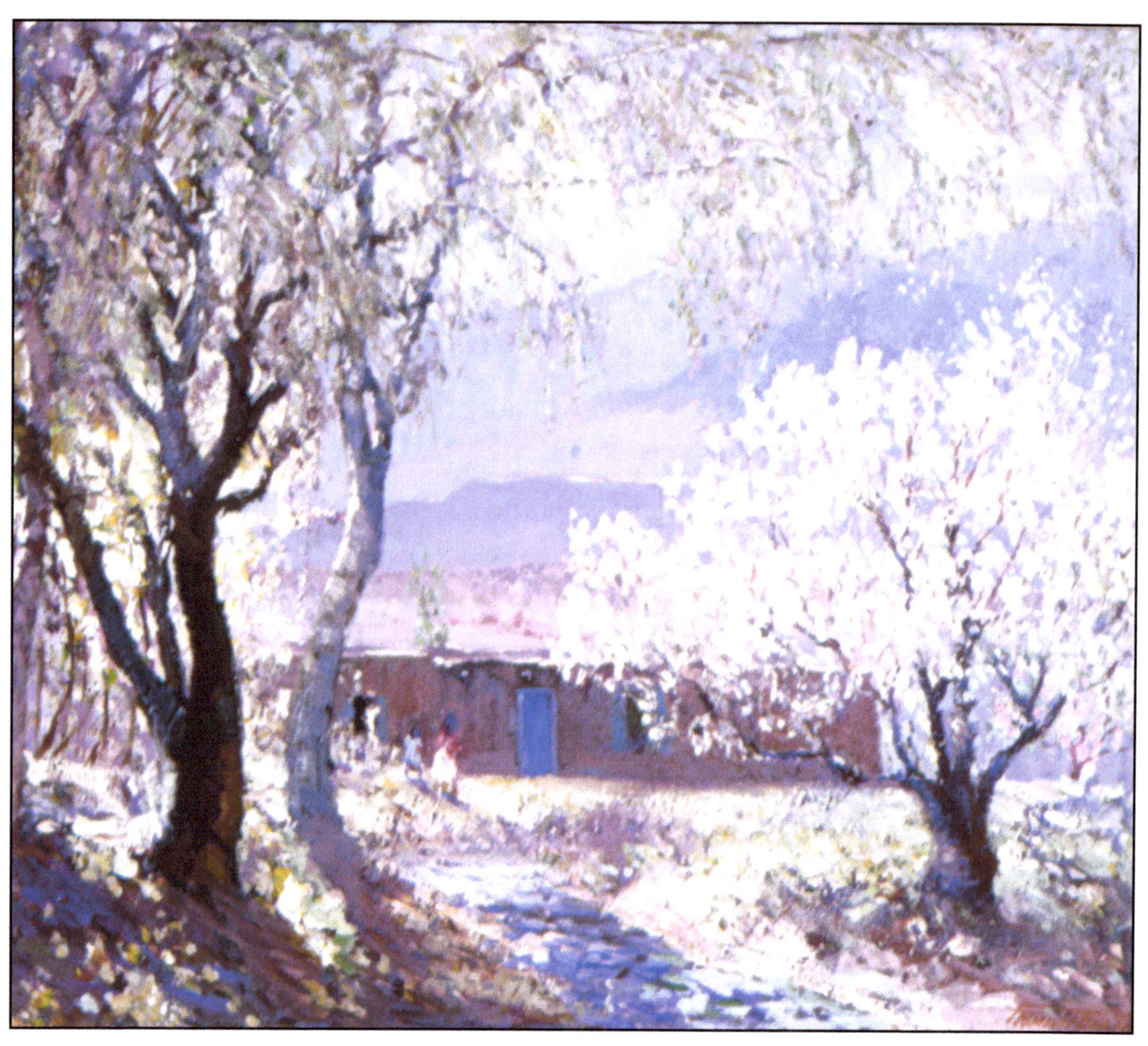

Acequia Madre, n.d., oil on masonite, 26 1/2 by 31 1/2 inches.
Collection of the New Mexico Museum of Fine Art, Santa Fe, New Mexico.
Bequest of the Estate of Ruby Cooper Pike, 1986.

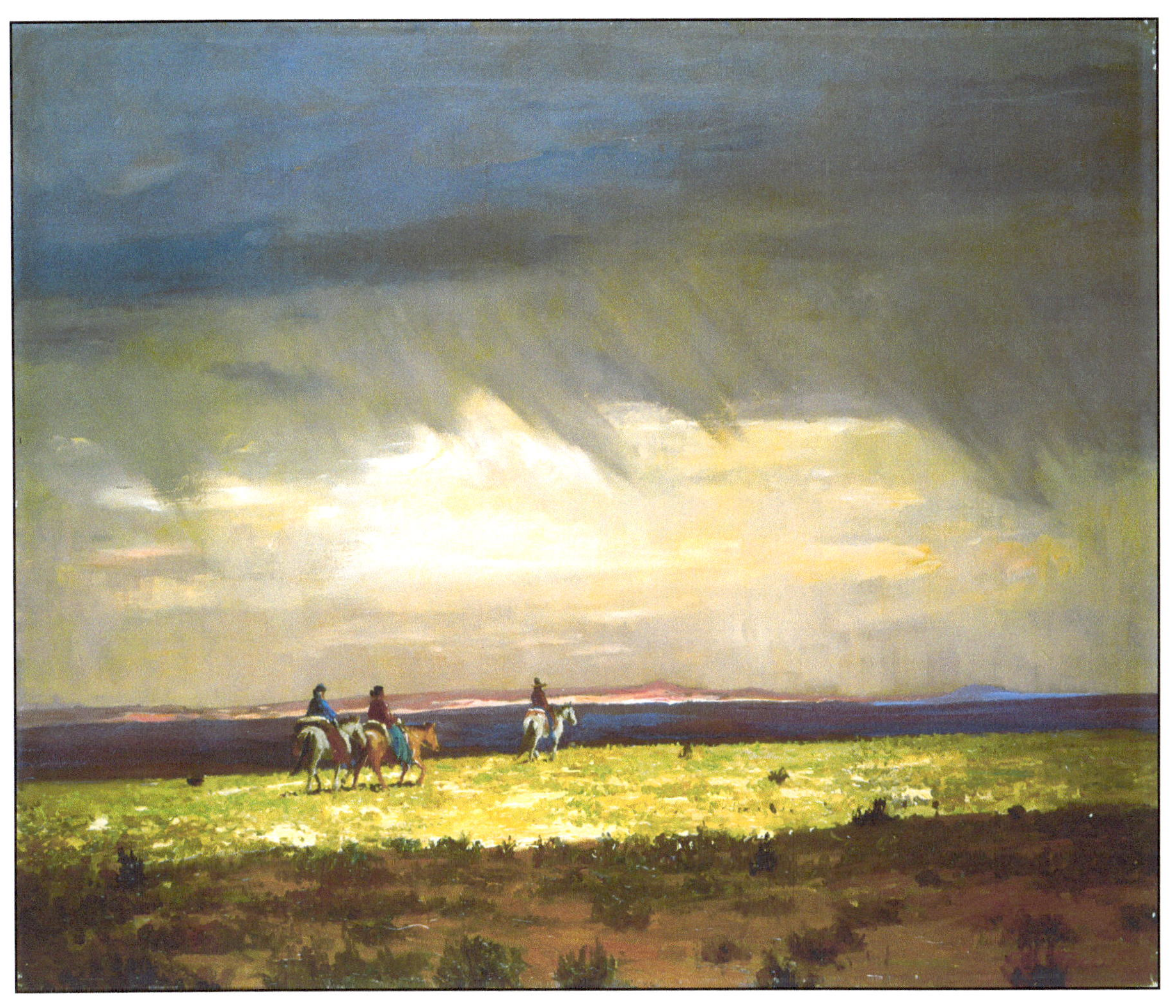

Walking Rain, c. 1951, oil on canvas, 24 x 30 inches.
Collection of Stark Museum, Orange, Texas.

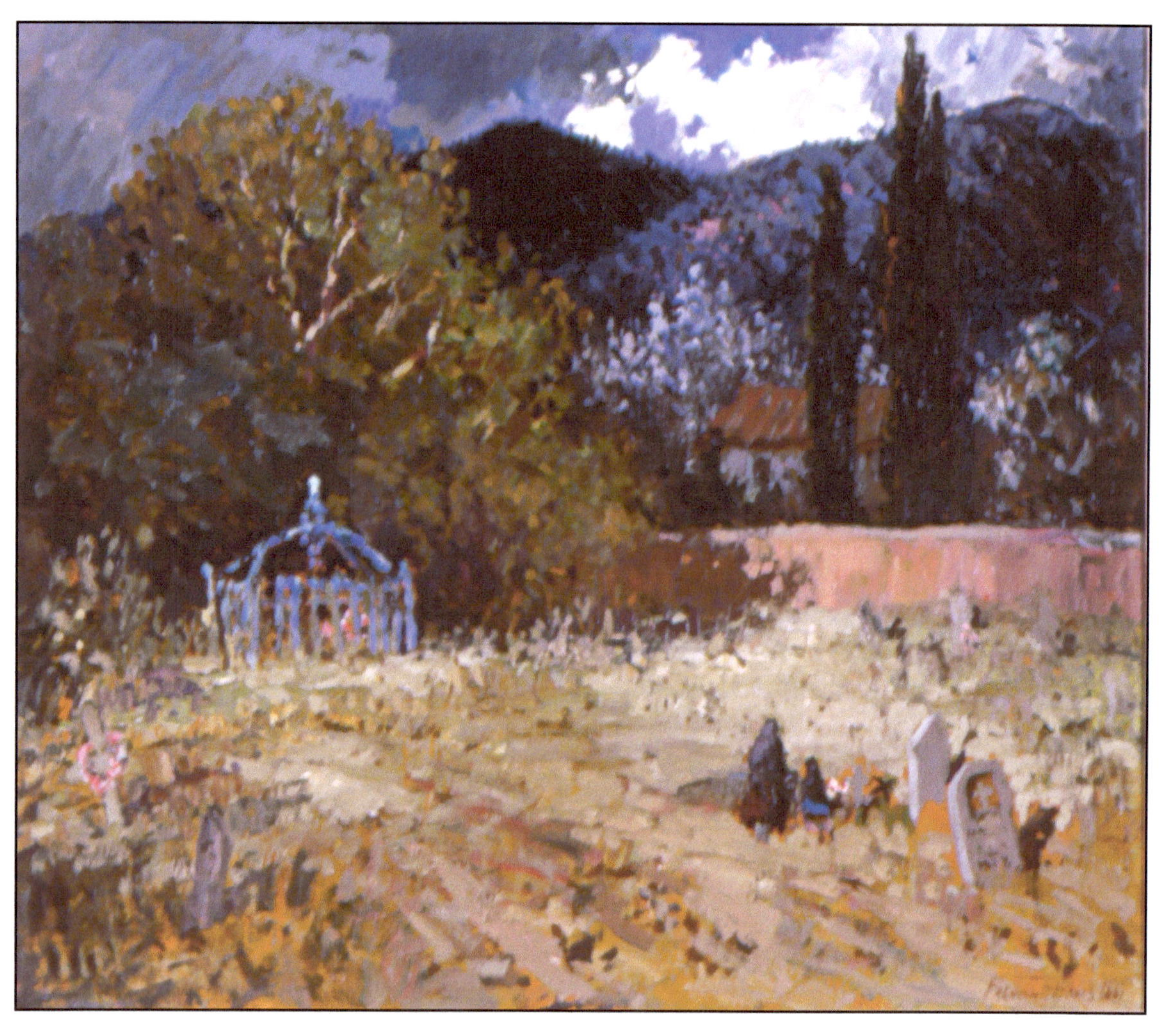

Campo Santo, 1966, oil on masonite, 27 x 32 inches.
Collection of the New Mexico Museum of Fine Art, Santa Fe, New Mexico.
Gift of Fremont F. Ellis, 1968.

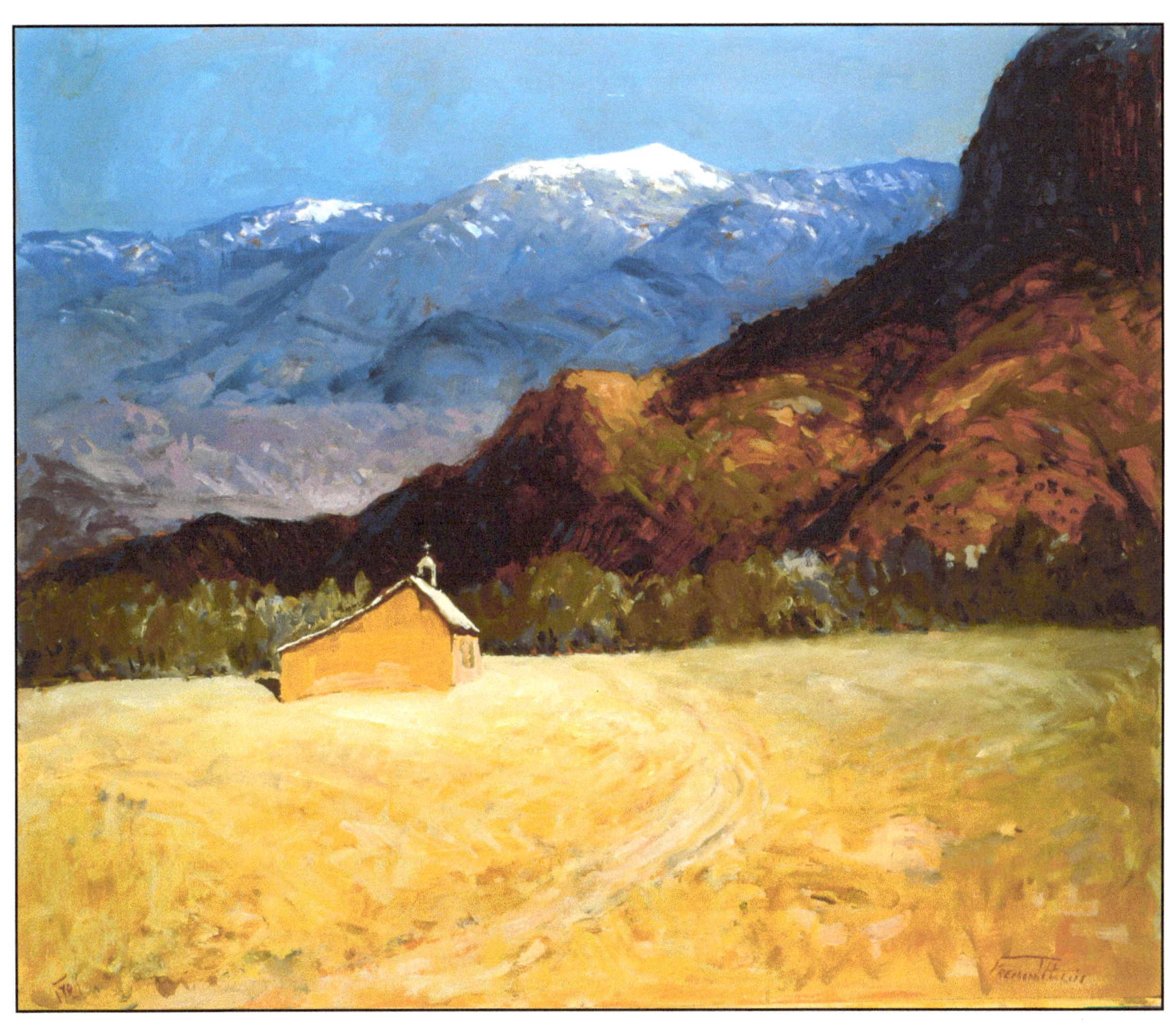

Capillita de Pajarito, 1970, oil on board, 27 1/8 x 33 1/4 inches.
Collection of the Stark Museum of Art, Orange, Texas.

IMAGES of the ARTIST

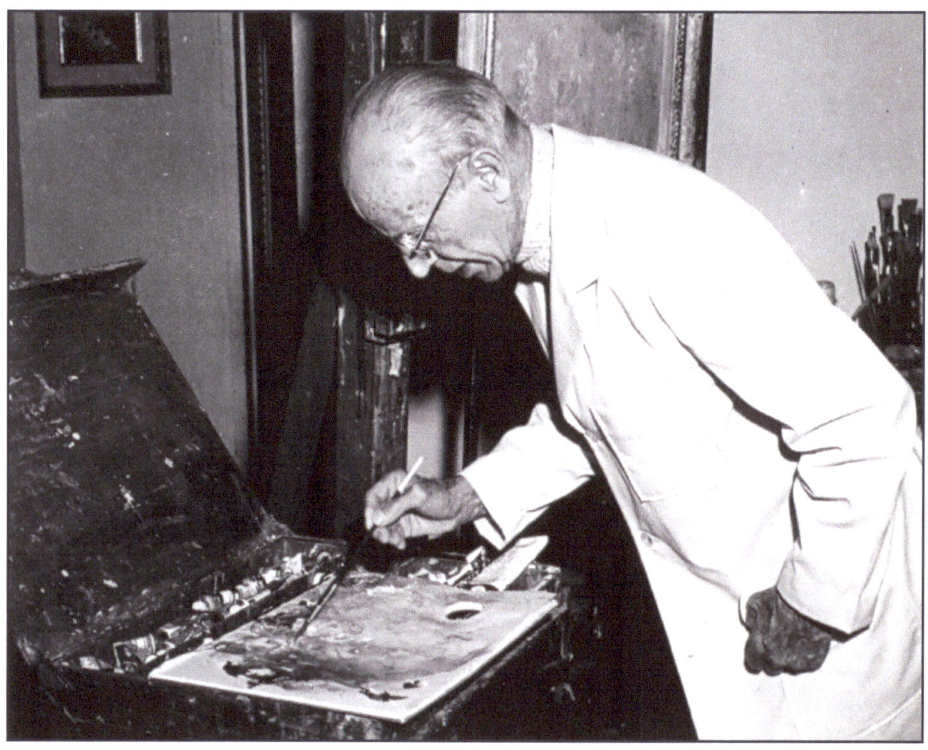

Ellis in his later years mixing paint in his studio.
Photograph courtesy of Bambi Ellis.

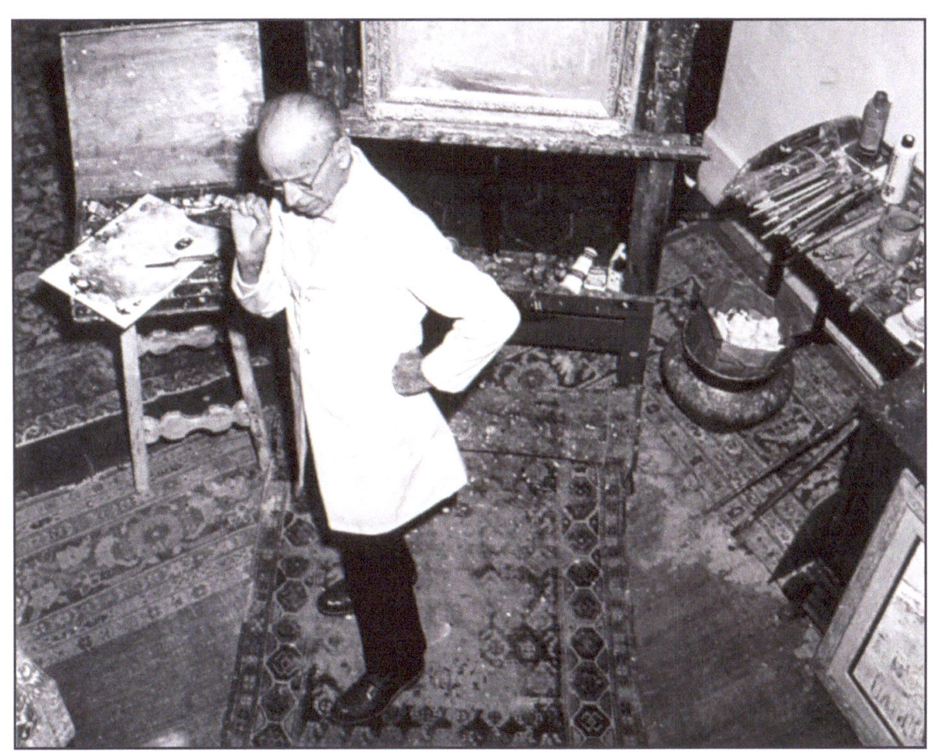

Ellis discussing his painting technique with a friend as he painted.
Photograph courtesy of Bambi Ellis.

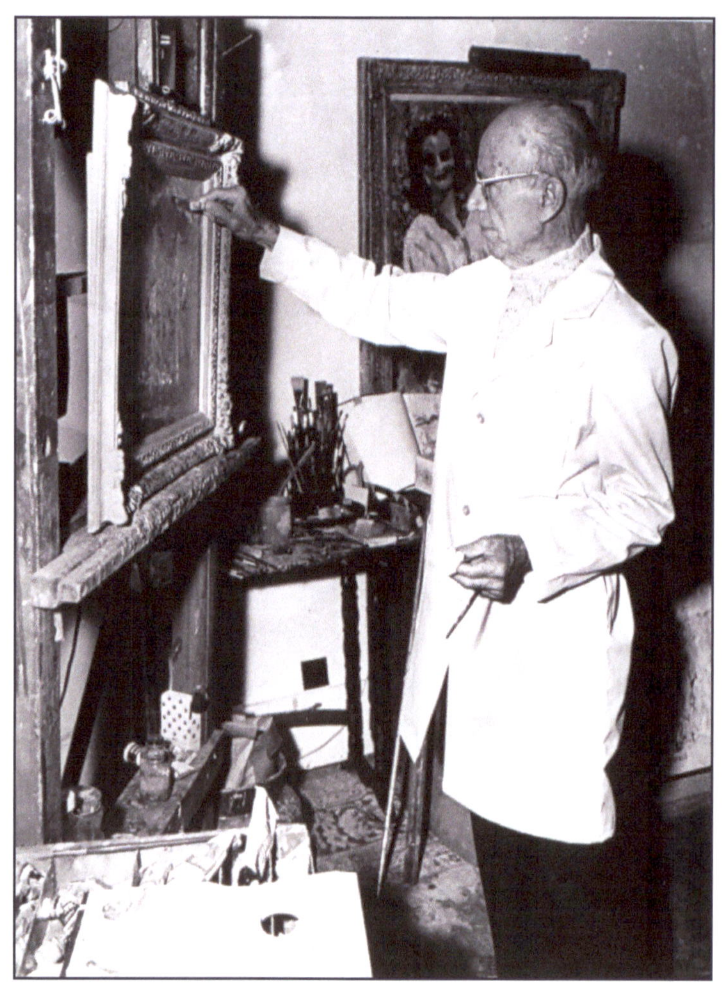

Ellis painted inside the picture frame to perceive an idea of how the finished painting would look.
Photograph courtesy of Bambi Ellis.

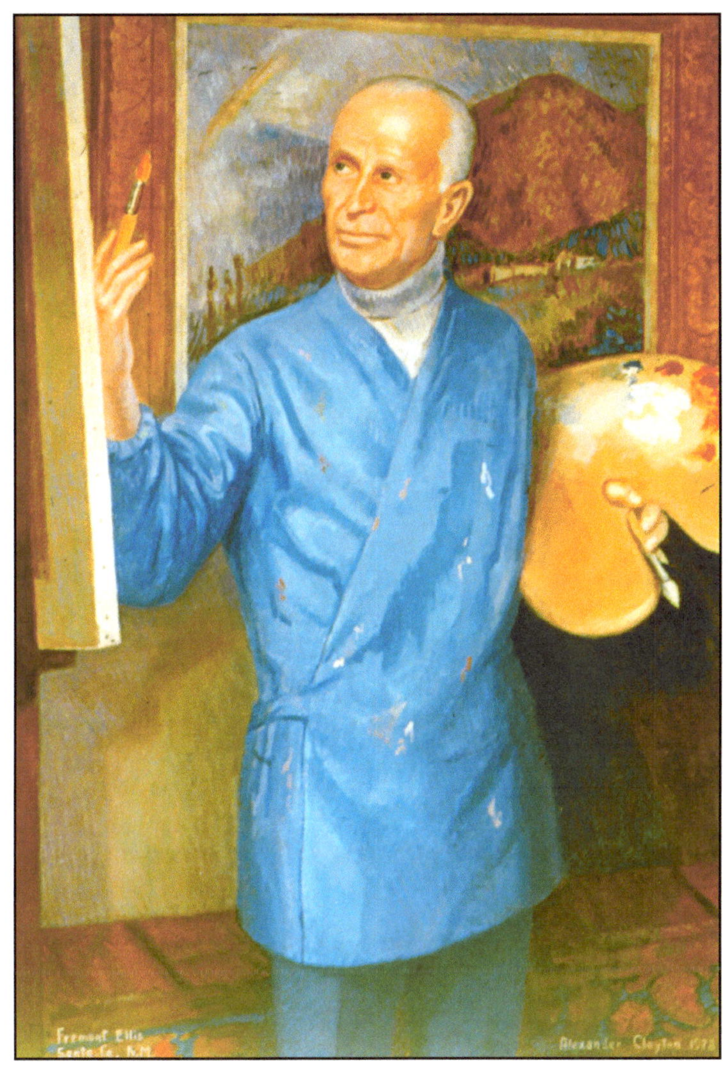

Alexander Clayton, *The Portrait of Fremont F. Ellis.* Clayton, a famous Dallas portrait painter, did the portrait for Ellis. Photograph courtesy of Bambi Ellis.

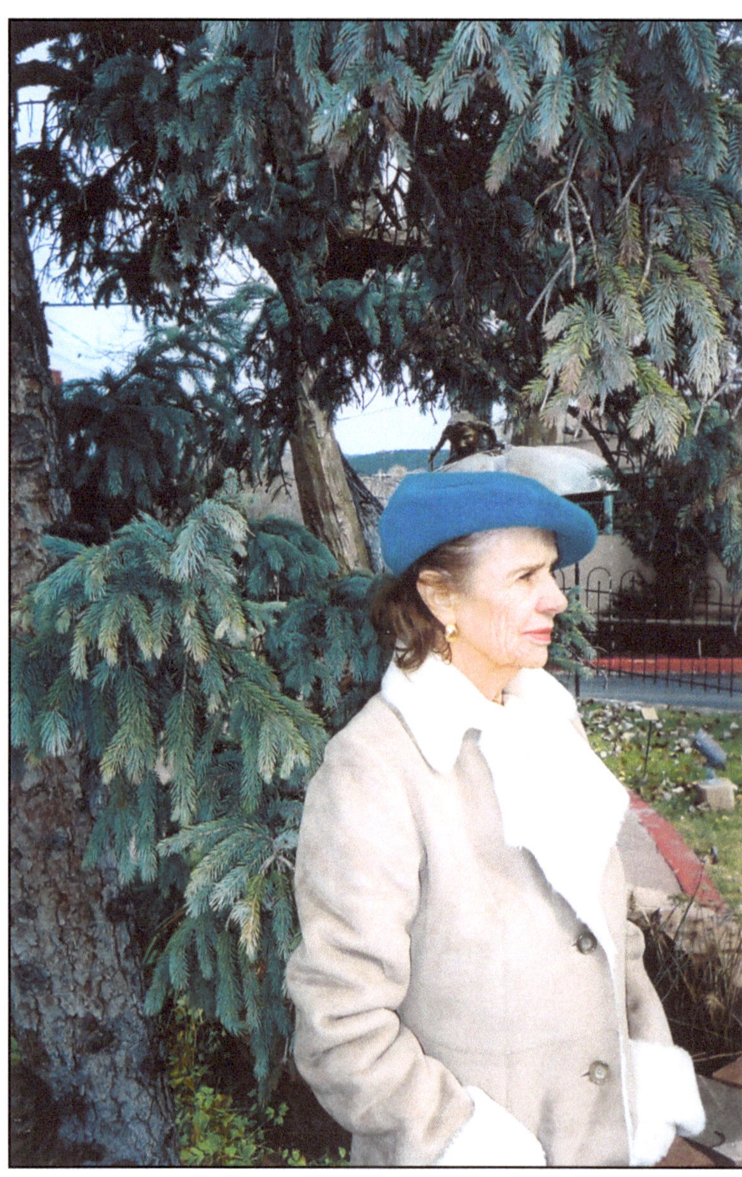

This book was wtitten with the help of Bambi Ellis, the daughter of Fremont F. Ellis.

www.ingramcontent.com/pod-product-compliance
Lightning Source LLC
LaVergne TN
LVHW071630100826
845154LV00007BA/124
* 9 7 8 1 6 3 2 9 3 4 2 6 0 *